CELEBRATING YOUR INTERCULTURAL MARRIAGE

CELEBRATING YOUR INTERCULTURAL MARRIAGE

Loving your differences and growing together

Louise and Les Isaac
with Rosalind Davies

First published in Great Britain in 2026

IVP1928 (An Imprint of Inter-Varsity Press)
Studio 101, The Record Hall, 16–16A Baldwin's Gardens, London EC1N 7RJ
www.ivpbooks.com

EU GPSR Authorised Representative
LOGOS EUROPE, 9 rue Nicolas Poussin, 17000, La Rochelle, France
Email: Contact@logoseurope.eu

British Library Cataloguing-in-Publication Data
A catalogue record for this book is available from the British Library

ISBN 978-1-78974-545-0
eBook ISBN 978-1-78974-548-1

10 9 8 7 6 5 4 3 2 1

Typeset by Fakenham Prepress Solutions, Fakenham, Norfolk NR21 8NL
First printed in Great Britain by Clays Limited, Bungay, Suffolk
eBook by Fakenham Prepress Solutions, Fakenham, Norfolk NR21 8NL

Produced on paper from sustainable sources

Inter-Varsity Press publishes Christian books that are true to the Bible and that communicate the gospel, develop discipleship and strengthen the church for its mission in the world.

IVP originated within the Inter-Varsity Fellowship, now the Universities and Colleges Christian Fellowship, a student movement connecting Christian Unions in universities and colleges throughout Great Britain, and a member movement of the International Fellowship of Evangelical Students. Website: www.uccf.org.uk. That historic association is maintained, and all senior IVP staff and committee members subscribe to the UCCF Basis of Faith.

For our children and grandchildren, who are living the blessing and richness of intercultural marriages and relationships. For this we are grateful to God.

Contents

Part 4
GOING FORWARD

Foreword

This is a beautifully crafted work of art around intercultural marriage. This work of art, to use the language metaphor of its writers in communicating key ingredients in an intercultural marriage, draws on over forty years of marriage experience.

I myself am in an intercultural marriage as a Yoruba Nigerian married to an English woman. Reading this book has transformed many aspects of my reflections on intercultural marriage. It has given me a new pair of lenses with which to view my intercultural marriage as a gift rather than a burden to carry. In essence, the strength and brilliance of this book is that it has been carved out by two people who walk this journey and understand with clarity the challenges involved.

Knowing the authors personally, and having been on the receiving end of their ministry and seen how they have impacted a lot of leaders and marriages, I can say that this book is a testimony to how God has used them in this area to encourage leaders in intercultural ministries and couples in intercultural marriages. This book, through practical experiences and outworking, narrates the journey of Uncle Les and Auntie Louise (as a good Nigerian boy, I cannot call them by their first names!). The exchange is therefore a work of art, giving us useful colours that have been tested by the authors through multifaceted experiences.

Perhaps people reading this might ask: why are the authors writing a book on intercultural marriage when they are both black? While they *are* both black, Uncle Les is Caribbean from Antigua and Auntie Louise is Black British of Caribbean background. They talk about this important distinction and how they define and understand intercultural marriage. You can have similar skin colour but be from different nationalities, ethnicities or cultures. This means, for example, a Ghanaian married to a Nigerian, although both black West Africans, have different cultural and ethnic groupings. Similarly, a white Australian and a white British, although having similar skin colour, have different nationalities and come from different continents and cultures.

Another major strength of this book is that while it encapsulates intercultural theology, it does so in an applied context that is not abstract thinking. In our current context of fragmentation, polarisation and division, there is a lot of talk around intercultural engagement in the areas of how we do church, how we do mission, how we engage with societal issues and how we can live in harmony. A major gap in our current intercultural conversation is regarding the family. The pattern of migration to the UK in the last decade has changed significantly. The 2021 census data reveals that white British ethnicity in England and Wales appears to be on the decline from 86% in 2011 to 81.7%, while other non-white ethnicity is on the increase from 14% in 2011 to 18.3%. One of the impacts of this increase in non-white ethnicity is the rise of intercultural relationships and marriages. For example, from the same census data, in England and Wales 10.1% (2.5 million) households in England and Wales have two or more ethnic groups represented. In cohabitation or marriage partnerships, 5.7% of households (1.4 million people) report different ethnicities. If there is a rise in intercultural marriages all across the UK, then it begs the question: how is the Church engaging and speaking into that? How is the Church preparing young people who might be interested in intercultural relationships and marriage?

We have people like myself speaking about the need to develop a new ecclesiology in Britain and to adopt the intercultural approach in our churches. We have other people who are helping us think through intercultural theology. Furthermore, we also have experts helping to engage intentionally in intercultural mission in a postmodern pluralistic society such as Britain. But we have few people speaking and writing about intercultural marriage. This is one of the significant gaps that this book is occupying, giving us a template for how we can develop and sustain intercultural marriage.

Marriage is not an easy business. Through marriage we learn a lot about ourselves, including the good, the bad and the ugly aspects of who we are. Through marriage, we can choose to become the best version of ourselves as the process of marriage refines us. Intercultural marriage takes all the above into another dimension, because of culture, worldviews, habits, choices and so on. This book addresses marriage, but more importantly it addresses the specifics of intercultural marriage from a Christian perspective. Those who are not Christian but from other faiths or none will still benefit from the wisdom in this book.

Finally, the questions and exercises throughout the book make it practical for couples to work through together. In addition, the book is not only for those already in intercultural marriages, but has many gems of wisdom for those starting out on this journey and the pitfalls to avoid. I would also recommend this book to those who lead or are seeking to develop intercultural churches, because it is useful to help couples in intercultural marriages in our churches, but also the metaphor of the Church being the body and bride of Christ means some of the principles in an intercultural marriage can be applied to an intercultural church.

Revd Dr Israel Oluwole Olofinjana
Director of the One People Commission
Evangelical Alliance

All names have been changed to protect identities. We are grateful for the enthusiastic and reflective participation of many couples in our marriage preparation sessions and in the different church congregations we have been part of. We are thankful to have been part of your faith journey and that you have been part of ours.

Welcome

The first years of our married life were a little turbulent. We agreed that we loved each other, but at the same time we were very frustrated with each other – our differences on all levels, our misunderstandings, our lack of communication and the absence of other people to help us. We kept silent about this trying time for two reasons. First, we didn't know who to speak to about it and, second, every other married couple around us appeared to be doing so well! We thought that if we were honest about our struggles, we would feel even more dysfunctional.

We had met, in our late teens, one Thursday evening at a church in Kentish Town, London. Les had recently become a Christian, finally finding answers to his questions in the Christian faith and leaving behind the Rastafarianism that he had practised for some years. Our friendship grew into love and six years later we got married. God graciously helped us to stay in love and stay prayerful and respectful of each other as we staggered through those first couple of years of marriage.

Life moved on and we became very involved in church leadership – facilitating missions, church growth and discipleship. These tasks turned our attention towards others in the Church and we got glimpses of couples in need of help, experiencing, we thought, some of what we had gone through.

Our natural response to these observations was marriage ministry, which began to develop organically as we opened our hearts to young couples and offered our home as a place to touch base, find openness, encouragement, good counsel and leadership. The desire of our hearts was to support marriages, by example, in prayer and through mentoring – and it still is. The extent of the turbulence we had been through alone, without support, was not necessary, we felt. We knew that if someone had just come alongside us to give us a steer and a word of encouragement, we would have managed far better. So we wanted to do that for others.

As the years went by, we became even more intentional in offering support by inviting groups of couples to our home for a meal and to talk about marriage – our marriage and the challenges we had experienced. Our openness and honesty drew couples from the Church and beyond. Many asked to meet with us to discuss their issues. Over the years, we have gone on to provide marriage seminars for church leaders, retreats and marriage workshops for married couples, and marriage preparation courses.

We have been together now for over forty years, as marriage partners and best friends, always responding to opportunities to share wisdom and support couples as best we can on their marriage journey.

This book is about marriage. And since it is all about being deliberate in understanding culture, we will begin by identifying *Christian* marriage as the distinctive culture that shapes our lives, our identity as writers and as husband and wife. A valued part of our married life has been the way we have embraced principles, instructions and practices from an ancient book of wisdom, the Holy Bible. We have done this because we are practising Christians. Although marriage pre-dates Christendom and exists in some form in most societies, any help to strengthen and maintain marriages, we think, is worthy of consideration. We are hopeful that the content that follows in these pages might help you in your intercultural marriage, whatever your religious persuasion and whether you are a person of faith or no faith.

This is a book about the joys and challenges of two becoming one, as two people from different cultural backgrounds begin a life together. Every individual carries traditions, rituals and attitudes around with them. We think of this in positive terms, as the unique combination of factors that make you 'you'. The cultural forces that have shaped your identity might have done so without you noticing, as you subconsciously inherited the customs of your family. Or you might have made some of these choices consciously yourself, perhaps rejecting some elements and accepting others.

We want to help you think about what happens when two people bring their different cultures together in marriage. Actually, a cultural mix is what happens in every marriage, but it's often not intentionally called out in the explicit way that we want to in this book. Every couple, even when both partners are from the same social, national and cultural group, will face some tensions that are a simpler version of what we are going to address here. Just think of the situation where one person's extended family spends a lot of time together and their partner has been brought up in a quiet nuclear family that keeps to itself. How will they handle this small difference when it spills into another area of their life or threatens to undermine one partner's identity and sense of self? Food, money, family, children, caring for elders ... there is a long list of the ways that cultural differences can affect everyday decisions in your married life.

Remember the ugly sisters in the fairy tale Cinderella? They are so determined to win the love of the prince that they try again and again to force that glass slipper onto their feet. We have written this book to make sure that as you step into the joy of married life, or you establish yourselves in the early years of your union, you don't find yourself looking at the glass slipper offered to you by your partner, wondering why it doesn't fit as you thought it would!

Cultural differences can easily be ignored and forgotten as couples prepare for marriage. Perhaps you are aware of some tensions but are not sure where they are coming from or what to call them. Cinderella's glass slipper is a symbol of the perfect union, but it's important to remember that sympathetic, supportive, difference-celebrating unions don't happen in fairy-tale ways! We have to work hard to achieve them.

Over the years we have talked with many couples, young and older, about the marriage challenges and issues they have faced. Many times, we have had to encourage them to dig deep to identify the cause of recurrent challenges. When they have done that, they have often found that the issues are rooted in cultural differences. Hence this book.

Our starting point as you join us for this journey is to encourage each partner to look closely at their background culture before looking forward to the future as part of a couple. Being deliberately aware of the different cultures that you and your partner bring, and the cultural choices that you want to make together, is the groundwork for a great intercultural marriage. Our aim is to help you make your own cultural blend, an agreement to hold on to some cultural distinctives and form a new cultural identity together.

In this book we present a basic theory about the importance of culture in every person's life. We encourage you to bring things to the surface with self-awareness so that together you can intentionally examine, include and exclude elements of your culture for the good of your ongoing relationship. Talking about cultural roots can help to formulate ideas about what you both want to see cultivated in your marriage and family life in the future.

An intercultural marriage is a work of art

As two individuals at the start of your marriage, you stand in front of a blank canvas. Each of you holds your own colour palette, made up of background cultural experiences and containing many different colours and shades. Looking closer, you can see that some paints are thicker than others, with a deeper and richer finish, as if they have been added to and pasted onto the palette several times. They were put on there long before the other colours. Some colours are vibrant, some take up more space on the palette, while some are paler and have been diluted. Some colours are similar to those on your partner's palette, with only a slight difference in hue, but for other shades there is nothing that comes close to a match.

In marriage, each of you stands an equal distance from a new canvas, the one that you make when you join your lives together. Both of you are at liberty to choose the colours, to use your brush and take part in the painting. Where will you begin to paint? Which colours will be most evident and which ones will fade out in the picture that you paint together? Which colour will be applied with the thickest brush strokes? Will colours be layered to create new ones and will these new ones be more vibrant or toned down?

This metaphor symbolises your intentional choice to create a new painting together and determine an outcome that you both regard as a work of art – your marriage, home and family.

Envisage your relationship as a creation of abstract art, full of colours. Some are bright and bold, while others are pale or more subtle. Each colour choice, brush stroke, wash and splash can be a conscious choice so that your joint artwork uniquely reflects your intercultural marriage creation. Each colour on your palette represents the various cultural components that each partner brings with them – as an individual with their own cultural background – into the marriage.

Does regard for culture matter when coming from different backgrounds? Do husbands and wives need to be intentional about what they carry forward from their culture and what they change or leave out to help make their marriage work well? We think so. An intercultural marriage can be a great marriage – a work of art – when crafted with conscious cultural sensitivity.

A book with self-awareness at its core

Self-awareness is a fundamental requirement of a healthy marriage. At the beginning of your marriage journey, we encourage you to analyse your art canvas and colour palette *as you find it at the moment.* We have planned this book so that in the first five chapters you have the opportunity to reflect on the ways that cultural colours have arrived onto your palette. This leads you to Chapter 6, which contains reflective exercises to help you examine and *know* the colours and shades of your own artwork as an individual. At the end of that chapter there is the opportunity for each of you to describe and label your paint palette as a way to launch and inspire your conversations.

Before this, Chapter 1 defines an intercultural relationship and invites you to think about the breadth of difference that two people might encompass. In Chapter 2, we outline the theoretical framework that we have adopted, within which we can organise our cultural colours into two groups: surface culture and deep culture. Chapters 3 and 4 take you through the sources of much of our cultural identity – family, role and gender expectations – and in Chapter 5, we look at the unwanted colours that come from adverse experiences and prejudice.

Up to this point, the chapters offer general advice with a Christian ethos, but as we move into Chapter 6 we begin to address the distinctives of an explicitly Christian marriage. We use Bible references and illustrations with the aim of sharing wisdom from our faith that can inform the challenges of life as a married couple, as well as those that might surface in relation to cultural difference. Appendix 2 complements this approach, and readers who would like to continue the Bible-centred focus can turn to 'The Bible and intercultural marriage'. In Chapter 7, we emphasise the basics of any good marriage. Continuing the artistic metaphor, we refer to this as the picture frame: a firm structure that holds the artwork and colours in place. The 'third strand' that is integral to our marriage, our Christian faith, is the subject of Chapter 8. We consider the kingdom culture, what it is and how it offers us a template for the priorities in our lives and marriages that is more important than any earthly culture.

Chapters 9 and 10 are designed to accompany you on your first steps in married life, as you become intentional culture creators together. We'll cover pre-marriage conversations and protocols and early-marriage changes, like moving to a different country and/or church. Finally, Chapter 11 describes the sources of support that might or could be available to you. We hope that this chapter helps both couples and churches to be aware of the need for support networks around intercultural marriages.

Throughout, we use examples and stories from our own experience, as well as those shared by other Christian couples (names and some details have been changed to preserve their anonymity), to help illustrate useful learning points and recognise culture-related experiences and ways they might be addressed.

The colours that have been poured onto our life canvas make us who we are as adults. Cultural input is a large and important part of our lives. It is the series of powerful learning experiences, from an early age, that shape our outlook. This cultural input combines with our personality to affect our 'output' in terms of behaviours, mindsets and attitudes to different situations. This may seem simplistic, but hopefully it is enough to help you appreciate that a good amount of colour-mixing and painting has happened over the years from birth to adulthood. Some streaks of colour will show through more than others, depending on learning recall and opportunities to apply the learning.

Thinking about what and why certain values are important to you will help determine whether you want them to have any status in your married life. This is what we think of as a three-step process: first, you will use your brush to lift colour from your personal canvas; next you will place these colours onto your palette; finally you will each choose the colours from your palette that you want to use to paint jointly onto your marriage canvas.

As you read this book, you will be invited to look closely at many aspects of your life and at parts of it that may have been ignored or pushed to the sidelines for many years. We encourage you to take the time, with the support of your partner (who is also taking this journey for themselves), to look carefully at the things that make you feel uncomfortable. It is important to recognise everything that has had some bearing on your life, and it is particularly important when something is uncomfortable or painful to be determined to learn from it rather than quickly pass it by.

We hope that this book will help you reflect as individuals and as a couple. We will guide you through reflective exercises that are designed to prompt you to think about what you are bringing to your relationship and what your union will look like. We encourage you to work independently and together on these exercises and be intentional about the conversations they open up. As you read on, we hope that the discussion and illustrations will resonate with you and provide encouragement, advice and (sometimes) caution for your own intercultural marriage journey.

Part I

THE MULTICULTURAL CONTEXT AND HOW YOU FIT INTO IT

1

What do we mean by intercultural marriage?

Intercultural marriage is a marriage between two people who have different cultural or ethnic backgrounds. It is not, as some might think, just about marriage between people of different skin colour or nationality. Culture is the experience of heritage, background and upbringing that forms the software running our current life experience. Cultural differences or similarities between a couple are deeper than skin colour and country of origin. For example, a couple with the same skin colour or nationality can be tripped up by assuming cultural sameness when, in fact, in many ways they are very culturally diverse – so much so that they become frustrated with each other's lack of understanding of what they 'should know' because of the assumptions they each make.

We are both of Caribbean heritage (Les was born in Antigua and Louise was born in London – children of the Windrush generation), but we have observed that in many dimensions we do not have a shared background cultural experience: some experiences are similar, but some are very different. We will share some of these stories as we go along. Suffice to say at this point, cultural sameness or differentness cannot be assumed because of colour or heritage. Finding out and sharing background stories is so important.

Louise recalls ... I had my first glimpse of cultural differentness a month after we were married, when Les came home from work and before taking off his coat he handed me an envelope.

'What's that?' I asked.

'It's my pay,' he answered.

I smiled, my mind promptly imagining all the luxuries I could buy with the cash in my hand. Noticing that I looked like the cat that'd got the cream, Les followed me into the front room, explaining that his gesture of handing over his pay packet was something he had seen his father do. His mother would then squirrel it away and apportion it to household necessities.

Both here in the UK and in Antigua, where he was born, Les had observed this behaviour between other husbands and wives in his family. That was why he had just done the same. I, however, had never seen this before. Crestfallen, I handed back the packet of money and for the first time in our marriage, we began a conversation about how, together, we would manage our finances.

That was my first experience in marriage of what is called cultural background difference in terms of gender role expectations.

Globalisation and the rise of intercultural marriage

The population of the UK is becoming more ethnically diverse. We are more likely than ever before, especially if we live in a city, to have neighbours who are of a different ethnic background from us. This is part of the increased movement and exchange of goods, services, technologies and cultural practices across the world.

One of the effects of this globalisation is that interaction between populations is promoted and increased. The growth of cities, the digital world and online dating are all indirectly accredited to globalisation and all of these factors have a bearing on the increased incidence of intercultural marriage.

Young adult city-dwellers, consequently, meet and interact with ethnic and cultural diversity often and at different levels. Most people who live in cities are accustomed to giving ethnic and cultural differences a cursory glance. They notice skin colour, style of dress, hair, head covering, language and accent – apparently superficial but important cultural identifiers. Interaction and dialogue in the workplace or educational settings also foster a level of cultural self-awareness and a consciousness of others' differentness, which may trigger cultural curiosity or indeed, cultural bigotry.

In 1967, when miscegenation laws were overturned in the United States, 3% of all newlyweds in the US were married to someone of a different race or ethnicity. Since then, intermarriage rates in the US and other countries have steadily climbed. In England and Wales, 10.1% (2.5 million) of households in England and Wales had two or more ethnic groups represented in 2021, according to the census of that year. In cohabitation or marriage partnerships, 5.7% of households (1.4 million people) reported different ethnic groups within the partnership.

Cosmopolitan churches

Churches often include people from different countries and backgrounds. This context inevitably brings together people of different cultures but the same faith. Christians coming together from different backgrounds share what we call a *kingdom-culture* dynamic. This is another paint on your palette. Do you paint this kingdom culture over your personal culture or mix the two together? We believe that faith is an addition that can help secure a special oneness as together you pursue your individual walk of faith. More about this later, in Chapter 8.

Multiculturalism lies within you

We're more likely to notice, if we were born in one country and then spent some significant time in at least one other, that we have a certain 'multiculturalism' that affects the way we do life. This is so by virtue of living and interacting closely with people of a different culture. Multiculturalism is generally defined as the presence of several distinct cultural and ethnic groups within a society. This diversity can impact community life for good, as the coexistence of different cultures, to some degree, affects individuals in most spheres of life. In fact, Christians, the Bible says, will ultimately live in a multicultural heaven. We believe that God's throne room will be full of ethnic diversity!

Intercultural couples actively reinvent themselves and develop hybrid identities that allow them to function in more than one cultural group or community. This self-consciousness hones their ability to slip seamlessly between cultures and becomes an asset to their relationship, removing feelings of awkwardness or a sense of displacement when they are with their spouse's family or friends.

Multiculturalism works for you both on a few other levels. If either of you is a second- or third-generation immigrant (there's an oxymoron for you), you will inevitably know and use many of the cultural norms of the society in which you are living. As a couple, therefore, it may be worthwhile asking yourselves, 'How much is too much?' or, 'How British do we want our marriage and home to be?' There is no suggestion of deficiency, superiority or inferiority in asking the question, but rather it is a way of evaluating the strength of colour each of the cultures brings into the marriage. It is a discussion to have early on, because your answer could have an impact on how you do life and family with your children in the future.

Class and culture

We said at the start of this chapter that intercultural marriage and interracial marriage are not the same thing. The term we are using, 'intercultural', is much broader than the term 'interracial'. The ideas in this book are based on the principle that partners with the same racial identity can still be poles apart culturally. We are used to hearing over-generalised terms, like 'Caribbean culture' or 'British culture', within which there is a huge range of cultural permutations that we think should be called out and valued. For this reason, we reflect on culture as a wide-ranging set of ideas and behaviours that can be usefully evaluated by couples who might appear (superficially) to come from a similar cultural background.

It is because of the breadth of our approach that we want to raise the idea that class difference can be one of the elements of cultural difference. Perhaps your marriage could be called 'cross-class' as well as 'intercultural'.

Class differences can be a source of tension and segregation, and perhaps, even more than cultural differences, give rise to antagonism. That may be because, fundamentally, the class system is a way of describing power inequalities. A partner who feels disempowered in their relationship may be consciously or subconsciously aware of class differences. Whether the cultural differences in your relationship originate in class, ethnicity or both, navigating and appreciating the differences is the focus of this book.

Social class, or in Asian societies the caste system, is a way that society organises people into groups based on crude factors like wealth and perceived value. You may not like the term or its judgements, but the simplistic categories of working class, middle class and upper class contain cultural ideas and behaviours that most people recognise and identify with. Class differences reveal themselves in a myriad of ways – for example, in attitudes to education and socio-economic factors – but can also be detected in speech and language variations and geographical mobility.

Use the questions overleaf to reflect individually on whether class differences are contributing to cultural differences in your relationship. Share your notes and reflections with each other.

- Based on the usually accepted hierarchy of social class, which class would you describe yourself as belonging to?
- What class-related conflict might be adding to the cultural differences in your relationship with your partner?
- What do you think is God's attitude to your differentness?

2

The 'iceberg model' of culture

'Culture' is the ideas, customs and social behaviour of a particular people group or society. 'Intercultural' is simply to do with the interplay of different people's cultures in relationships. This theoretical outline will hopefully provide you with a backdrop for thinking about your own cultural make-up and the impact each element of it has had, and continues to have, on your life.

The 'iceberg model' of culture was developed by Edward T. Hall in his 1976 book *Beyond Culture*, and it is a theory formulated originally in relation to organisational culture. Hall suggests that 'organisational culture is like an iceberg ... it has the characteristic of being highly disproportionate in its actual visibility'. He goes on to point out that the least visible elements of a culture, below the surface, are the most dynamic in terms of affecting an organisation's function and output.

An individual's culture is, similarly, like an iceberg in that only a small part of it is obviously visible (above the water line). The visible, tangible parts of a person's or society's culture form a small proportion of their make-up. Surface culture is easy to see. Below the surface of the water, however, is the greater mass of the iceberg. Likewise, the cultural norms that form us on a deeper level are more difficult to see at first glance but are very much present and impactful in a person's life. Hall calls this below-the-surface culture 'deep culture'. This deep culture manifests as behaviours, attitudes, values and beliefs that have been formed by the essential customs and conventions of a society or community a person has lived in from an early age.

Anthropologists agree on three characteristics of culture, Hall says in *Beyond Culture*: it is not innate, but learned; the various facets of it are interrelated (you touch a culture in one place and everything else is affected); it is shared and in effect defines the boundaries of different groups. Culture is the most obvious aspect of human life, influencing behaviour in deep and subtle ways, and yet, Hall suggests, it is taken for granted.

It is this unseen set of cultural norms that we will focus most of our thinking on. The interaction of people in a marriage relationship involves a blending or negotiating of what Hall calls 'deep culture' material to make the ongoing relationship work well. We will elaborate on this theory and also use our metaphor of colours and artwork to illustrate it as we go along.

Surface culture

Hall refers to surface culture as the cultural elements of the individual that are easy to see or are more visible. These include food, music, language, festivals, dress/fashion, the arts.

In the artwork metaphor, we liken surface culture to foreground colours that are bright, bold and obvious but also delible (easily deleted or changed because, when painted on, they never dry completely). In other words, surface culture can, overall, be adjusted or changed completely by an individual. Surface culture is more likely to change according to the different seasons of married life; for example, when you are young, when you have children, when you are older, when you are financially stable and so on. It is also more likely to change according to the physical and social context you find yourself in; for example, 'appropriate' dress may require that you do not wear traditional attire as often as you would like, either because the weather is too cold for it, or you would not fit in with a social group the way you would like to.

Living in cosmopolitan cities has encouraged many to engage in 'culture-dipping', whereby people choose a fusion of surface-culture elements from the variety they are exposed to, based on whatever they find appealing. For example, the dreadlocks hairstyle was originally a surface cultural identity statement of Rastafarians (a Caribbean religious sect). Today dreadlocks are worn by many as an African/Caribbean hairstyle with no religious connotations. They are also sometimes worn by men and women from other ethnic groups.

Surface-culture attributes are things like dress, food and language. They are important personal identity markers, and are often more vibrant colours but, as we have said, they are colours that never fully 'dry'. In other words, they are more changeable.

Deep culture

Hall refers to deep culture as those cultural elements in a community that are more difficult to see, or are less visible. We refer to them here as 'background colours'. These include:

- *Beliefs*: the ideas, philosophies and religious thought common to a community that govern interactions between the community, their god(s) and other people groups.
- *Values*: what a society collectively agrees about what is good or right, bad or wrong. It can also define what a 'successful' life looks like.
- *Ethics*: the generally accepted morality endorsed by the community, usually emerging from commonly held beliefs and values.
- *Customs*: the widely accepted, traditional ways of behaving that are unique to a particular society.
- *Traditions*: the beliefs, values, ethics and customs passed down from one generation to the next, established as customary patterns of thoughts and behaviour.

Probably one of the first things you will notice about these categories is how intertwined the elements are. The definitions cross over into each other. This simply serves to demonstrate how complex we all are and how full we are of the stuff we have learned, imbibed or been trained in – most of it unknowingly!

Under one or more of these core deep-culture headings are:

- gender role attitudes and expectations
- approaches to courtship and marriage
- notions of modesty and beauty
- attitudes to age
- work ethic
- notions of cleanliness and good manners
- communication styles and rules, such as personal space protocols, appropriate body language, displays of emotion, gestures, touch, eye contact
- ideas about child-rearing
- ideas about the importance of family
- humour, slang and idioms.

Our culture gives us a varied palette of colours that informs us and helps us to play out our personal and community identity. We use these colours in our lives all the time, having learned them in our early years. Cultural identity is really the combination of our surface cultural expressions and our deep cultural experiences. It is a collection of things that say, 'This is me.' In other words, these are the things that have contributed to our life to make us the person we are.

This 'colouring' affects our sense of self but also of belonging and connectedness to others. Being with others of a similar hue, whose canvasses have similar colours and markings to our own, gives us a sense of rootedness. Our background colours had already been splashed or carefully painted onto our personal art canvas long before we were able to consciously make life choices about them. They were painted on by adults who held a colour palette of cultural mores – the characteristic customs and conventions of the community or society in which we grew.

A person's background, in Western societies, is often a layered fusion of several cultural influences because, as a child grows, they are exposed to other individuals or groups with different cultural experiences. This is the dominant societal cultural context into which a child is born and spends their formative years. Society's impact upon a young person cannot be overstated, especially if the young person moves to another country and therefore assimilates, to some degree, other cultural norms.

Referring to yourself as Black British, for example, is generally regarded as a political statement. However, it is also an acknowledgement of the cultural heritage of an African or Caribbean background and the upbringing that relates to it by being born in Africa or the Caribbean, or by being children of migrants from these places. The point is that elements of the background culture are lived out in a current British context. The same is true of Asians, other ethnic groups and all second- and third-generation people groups living in Britain or many other non-Western nations. Shades of background cultural colour are always carried, and layers of new and current cultural exposure are added. The colour blending in an individual that has already happened before a couple meet is quite remarkable.

Awareness of the cultural colours that have made you who you are, up to the point at which you choose to get married, is important. Seeing your own multi-coloured palette is the starting point for you and your spouse to be intentional about what you want your marriage relationship and future life together to look like, on your shared marriage canvas.

These colours represent your deep culture. Deep-culture shades create the atmosphere of the picture. They are an important 'wash' over the whole canvas of your relationship. They affect the atmosphere of your marriage and your home.

Background colours are largely indelible because they were painted onto our canvas a long time ago by significant adults and experiences. In other words, they were learned from an early age and therefore represented the 'normal' and expected cultural behaviour for us as young people. We often have to think carefully to identify these deep-culture features and how they have influenced our behaviour and attitudes. It can be hard to identify them, because they are so normalised. Background colours can be lightened (this may be something we do consciously when a cultural experience has had a negative impact on our identity), but the colour cannot be removed from our own palette completely, because it is a part of our lived experience. Therefore, dialogue about our background colours is so important.

Cultural profiles

Cultural self-awareness is one of the most positive and affirming things a couple can take into their marriage. You have all of this to unpack, discuss and work through in order to paint a shared cultural canvas that you both want and which complements your marriage. It will have a colour scheme that you both like and want to journey with at the start of your marriage. A work of art like this requires that you invest in pockets of 'talk time' during which you look at and agree about which parts of your individual culture you both wish to include as foreground and background colours.

In our experience, a good intercultural marriage is one in which both partners have done some inner work. Intercultural marriage is an opportunity to choose the colours from your palette and to share and mix colours on a shared canvas. We encourage you to avoid letting this happen in an unconsidered and haphazard way. Instead, we advocate for the joy of this process as a unique experience of two people becoming one through sharing the diversity of their cultural experiences.

As we unpack the artwork metaphor, you will see that each of us has a variety of colours on our palette – some deep, strong colours; others weaker and lighter. Some will be in the foreground and others in the background of the picture that we will make. These colours have been transferred to our palette by our personal life experience. This transfer of colour from personal canvas to palette then to another's canvas or a shared canvas is an inevitable consequence of personal relationships.

Martha is a successful HR consultant in her late thirties. We asked her to describe the colours on the palette of her life.

> One of the strongest 'cultural colours' in the early years of my life was academic excellence, ambition and success. This is a dark, background shade on my palette, layered over and over by my parents' Indian culture. Academic education was paramount and this continued after we moved to Manchester when I was ten years old. Playtimes at home were limited, and extra-curricular activities after school were never bought into. My evenings and weekends were filled with homework (set by teachers), home learning (set by Mum or Dad) and private tutoring. As a teenager planning to go to university, I never dared to ask for a gap year, because I felt it would be met with disapproval.
>
> When I started work, I decided to cut myself some slack and lighten this colour. I allowed myself two years off before doing my masters degree. I also 'gifted' myself downtime with new friends and hobbies and life experiences that I realised I had missed out on because the push for academic excellence was so strong in my family.
>
> When I married and had children, I chose to mix the colour I had experienced with my husband's colours. His idea of academic success was more relaxed, with an adventure-seeking approach. His idea of education was much broader

than mine had been and he wanted our family life to contain varied non-academic experiences and expeditions, which he regarded as memorable and valuable in his formative years.

I am not denying the benefits of the strong background family colour that I grew up with, but I have chosen to lighten the colour and welcome the colours of the different norms of my husband's culture.

My parents died when I was in my twenties and I noticed a new colour appearing in my life as friends filled the gap that my parents left. This friendship group was the source of much support, laughter and honesty, and it became a formative part of my early adult life. Although I am now married, the friendships are still strong and, I would say, I have carried the importance of giving and receiving friendship onto my paint palette. It is splashed over the top of all other colours.

I often speak to family members in my native Bengali tongue. I can switch into the language easily, and it holds great value for me at this stage of my life, affirming my cultural identity and my parents' love and intentional nurturing by teaching us our native language; so I would say that that colour has now deepened.

Hospitality is a custom that I want to maintain, but I know that my husband doesn't value it in the same way. I'd say that this is a background colour for me, but it doesn't have the same vibrant depth that it used to have.

Also on my palette is traditional dress. I like to wear saris, although the happy memories of family occasions when I would wear them are tinged with the more recent scars from the negative comments I got from work colleagues once when I wore a sari to an important conference. I would love this colour to be stronger, as it once was, but at the moment it is quite a light shade; I can hardly see it.

Most people don't take the time to weigh up their experiences and make considered decisions about the norms and traits they want to perpetuate and those they don't. When someone uses the phrase 'It was good enough for me, so it's good enough for them', it demonstrates the ease with which we can transfer a cultural experience wholesale without thinking about the impact it has or whether it translates to a different context among different people. By reading this book, and engaging in its reflective exercises, you are recognising that paint palettes are the place for evaluating colours, mixing shades and even creating brand new ones.

Having begun to think about the potential impact of culture on our relationships, we hope that you will want to reflect on your own (multi)cultural profile. Part 2 contains reflective exercises through which both of you can continue to focus on the deep and surface cultures that you bring into your marriage. Chapters 5 and 6 direct you to the image of an empty paint palette for you to annotate, which you can find on page 161. Here you can add the colours of your life so far as a way to visualise your cultural differentness before creating the shared artwork of your marriage.

Part 2

INHERITED COLOURS

3
Family colours

Parents and significant family members have played an important role in the acquisition of our cultural norms during our formative years.

'If you can't hear, you will feel!' is a phrase that many Caribbean-heritage people have heard and understood from an early age. It means that if you refuse to adhere to verbal instructions or messages of caution that are given for your benefit, you might experience a mishap. This could be in the form of a smack, to deter you, or an actual accident. Either way, it refers to an experience the child will hopefully learn from without too severe consequences.

Each culture group has its ways of teaching its children important cultural norms: through storytelling, the use of idioms, practical examples and training, exposure to experiences or support while learning. The child who learns well receives praise and encouragement. Not getting it right attracts further help and encouragement to improve. Being regarded as 'a good girl' or a 'good boy' is the aspiration of the child. It sends the message that the behaviours, attitudes, values, beliefs and other cultural materials have been learned well and they are deserving of the accolade.

Parents and other significant adults all have a part to play in forming the child's cultural template as it becomes part of their identity. In other words, parents have the right to paint on a child's canvas the surface and deep colours necessary to enable them to fit into society, forming their identity and sense of belonging.

A parent's role in forming and culturally crafting the child ends when the child becomes an adult.

Transition to adulthood

Like most parents, we gave our children more and more responsibility and independence as they neared adulthood. We encouraged them in such a way that they could eventually trust their own judgements, ask for advice and step into adulthood knowing that they would be appropriately supported by us.

When our son and daughter became young adults, we felt our role was to ask questions that would encourage them to think beyond their limited knowledge and immediate circumstances, and then be available to give information and advice as required. We learned to trust their choices and decisions and, more so, trusted God with their lives – as we had done through their childhood. We encourage you to do the same if you become parents.

The role and relationship of parents to their adult sons and daughters, therefore, should be different from that of a parent to their children. This is where the issue becomes relevant to the couple embarking on marriage: sons, daughters, mothers and fathers need to get their heads around this truth before the younger generation enter marriage, to avoid upset or cultural impositions. Most cultures place parents in very high esteem – sacred texts do too. Yet setting boundaries for parents, family and friends is also referred to in Scripture and is prudent in marriage. In other words, parents painting on *your* marriage canvas is not allowed!

We want to share some biblical principles that can help to clarify your position as adult sons and daughters in relation to your parents. This is to make clear what your starting point as a couple should be and to avoid 'colour-splashing' by parents.

Child to adult: the biblical model

No longer a child

Marriage is a line in the sand for most people in most cultures. It's the point at which, even with co-habitation and the trend for delayed marriage (in the UK, the average age for men and women to marry is in their late thirties), many families recognise a definitive shift in loyalty and roles. The impact is not just for your parents and elders, but for you too. After all, marriage is for adults who are assumed to have a certain level of maturity and responsibility so that they can start a new household without their parents' involvement.

The transition is not always smooth. Some parents have a problem with accepting that their child has become an adult. Of course, this is further aggravated if that 'child' chooses a partner and decides to get married. The gradual change in the relationship between parents and sons and daughters, and the necessary acceptance that the nurturing and imparting parental role has ended, can be challenging.

Leaving and cleaving

As a legal and emotional step, marriage is a contract, we believe, that excludes any third person from that relationship of intimacy. Mentally and emotionally leaving Mum and Dad – changing those relationships – must be a conscious step away from your original nurturers and teachers so that you can embrace or cleave to your spouse. *Leave and cleave* is language that comes from the Bible, and it refers to the process of changing your loyalties and boundaries as you leave one family to start another and join yourself (cleave) to your spouse. The significance of leaving is not necessarily a physical move (you may well need to live with parents for a time), but it is a psychological, emotional and spiritual move away. Our highest commitment and loyalty must be to our spouse once we are married. Remind yourself of this often.

Respect for parents

Obedience to parents is required of children. However, obedience to parents is not required of adults. As an adult you may seek out or hear your parents' advice, but you are under no obligation to follow it. You may respectfully decline!

Parents who get upset when their offspring don't take their advice do not fully appreciate that their relationship to an adult son or daughter is one of adviser and not one of an authority figure who gives orders. As an adult, you can take their advice or leave it, because it is your job to form your own opinion as to what you should do. Sometimes adult sons and daughters do not help the transition from child to adult, because they themselves are not clear about the changes. In marriage, spouses can be unknowingly brought into the confusion.

Honouring a good and faithful parent is a lifelong responsibility for each of us. It means to confer an important, serious level of respect in what we say and do, to and for our parents. So, although there is a point at which we no longer have to obey our parents, there is never a time when we should stop giving them honour or respect. There are ways of saying no respectfully.

Reflect on your own context: whose voices can you hear?

When a personal and romantic relationship develops, the couple have to work out their compatibility. Think back to the early days of your relationship. Were you aware of each other's nationality, heritage and/or background, social class, ethnicity, country of origin? Perhaps it was all or some of these. The questions you probably asked yourselves were: can we make our differentness complementary or not? When we get past the novelty of our relationship, will this relationship go further for longer? Beyond this, however, you may have had to respond to a variety of reactions to your relationship. This is another way in which intercultural marriage demands attention and awareness.

Love is blind, so the saying goes, but most of your family and friends will see the 'colour' differences in your relationship. You may be well aware of what others think of your relationship, or it may be something that has not been voiced in your presence.

We have curated a range of reactions and assumptions that might surface when your nearest and dearest realise that your relationship is serious and heading towards marriage. We encourage you to take some time to reflect on the family and friends who are speaking about and into your relationship, and think about the voices that matter to you. If a significant person in your life has an opinion about your relationship, it will be doing one of two things: creating stress or reducing stress. Their voice will be either making you question your future path or encouraging you to follow your path. It is likely that you have already spent or are going to spend a lot of energy talking to that person and explaining your feelings to them. You will probably be keen to make it clear how much you have thought about your decision. If that significant person is not on your side in this conversation, you are probably working hard to win them over. It's also possible that the relationship has come under such pressure that it has broken down. There comes a time when you and your partner have to decide that you have done all you can and it is time to withdraw from this demanding conversation. We suggest that if you do reach this stage, you turn to other people, peers or family members, and listen and talk to them. Other people's opinions matter to us, especially if they come from those we love and respect. Listening to these people, whether they have a positive view or a negative view, is a way in which we show that respect.

Simon did everything he could to build a relationship with Shola's mother, his future mother-in-law. But she wasn't having any of it! In her mind, he did not fit the bill on several counts, professionally, financially, ethnically and culturally. Shola's mum had 'more suitable' young men lined up for her only daughter.

In Shola's mind, her mum had no regard for compatibility or love. 'That will come later,' was her mum's view. The conversation became repetitive over the course of a year. Shola and Simon therefore decided to move on and make their wedding preparations, supported by friends, but hopeful that there might be a change in her mum.

Here are some of the voices you may have heard.

'You've decided to get married! Wow, that's great! You go well together.' The voice of celebration and joy that recognises you are two people who can make each other happy.

'You've thought about your differences and decided you're right for each other.' The pragmatic voice that recognises you have thought ahead and been proactive in talking about your different cultures.

'There are other intercultural couples around you whose relationships appear to be working well; you can learn from them and use them as a support.' The voice that encourages you to observe and connect with other couples who are your peers, knowing that through these relationships you will learn about the joys and challenges that more established intercultural couples have experienced and this will inform your own marriage journey.

'We'll be on hand to help you if we can.' The supportive voice that acknowledges the challenges for any marriage.

'You've chosen someone who is not like us!' The voice of prejudice and discrimination, which may demand reserves of patience and forgiveness from you.

'This will look bad for me as your parent!' The voice of a proud parent who feels that your marriage is partly a reflection of them, their parenting and their status.

'Here comes trouble. The family won't accept this.' The voice that expresses concern for your partner's place in the wider family unit. Whatever you feel for each other, this voice says that there are other people involved.

'Do you know what you're letting yourselves in for?' The voice of fear that says your partner is not good for you. There are worries about the potential difficulties the relationship may bring, both within the family and outside.

Truth be told, every marriage has its challenges, however culturally similar or dissimilar you may be. Your love and loyalty to each other and your Christian faith can help you stay together, but it is important to pre-empt those voices and conversations that are underpinned by the idea of 'trouble ahead'. We recommend that you welcome and instigate explicit conversations with loved ones to show that you recognise the realities of bigotry and acknowledge that cultural differences will present some challenges that need to be worked on. You will be able to say that your friendship, love and commitment to each other are your greatest motivation for and in your marriage. Remember that all marriages are a work in progress: addressing cultural differences when necessary is a part of the way in which you will make progress as an intercultural couple.

As a couple, therefore, there is some wisdom in trying to demonstrate, to those who are concerned, that you are in love but not colour blind! In fact, on the contrary, you are both culture conscious and aware of how some of your differentness might play out in your marriage – by choice and by default. Spend some time reflecting together on the voices that are expressing opinions about your relationship and ask yourselves the following questions:

- Who is expressing an opinion about your relationship right now?
- Of these voices, whose matters most to you?
- What is the point of view of the person you have identified?
- How does this feel to you? Is it helpful or unhelpful?

If you are a Christian couple, it is important that you are clear about the Bible's teaching on your intercultural relationship. Simply put, nowhere in the New Testament does God instruct anyone to reject a potential marriage partner on the grounds of ethnic origin. Instead, Scripture encourages people to choose based on their commitment and devotion to God. You can read more on this in Appendix 2, where there is a discussion of Old and New Testament references.

Family interactions

Wider family relationships are an area of life frequently mentioned as a source of the greatest relief and the greatest grief! Relief, when aunties and grandparents willingly turn up and are helpful. Grief, when there is misunderstanding or conflict.

How we do family relationships is often affected by our upbringing and exposure to immediate or extended family. We often, therefore, come together in marriage from different places in terms of background family experience and expectations.

Newly married couples often interface with family members with all sorts of expectations, but just as importantly, family members have expectations of the couple. Couples from similar background cultures are faced with largely *known* expectations. Couples with apparently dissimilar backgrounds have a 'leeway of uncertainty' – an allowance of freedom – after marriage, when family weigh up how to relate to them as a couple, before fixing their expectations.

The spectrum of family cultural expectations

We suggest that families fall in different places along a spectrum. Take this opportunity to think about the different shades of your experience of family life, and plot yourselves along the spectrum in the table below. You can then compare your different positions and begin a conversation about how these colours will affect your shared marriage canvas.

For example, is your family a 'closed' family or an 'open' family? As a couple, we were poles apart in this respect.

Les recalls ... I had lots of contact with cousins, aunties and other relatives in my home. This group of people interacted freely with my mum, dad and four siblings; sleeping over, eating together – all of it was unplanned. This was very much my home life in Antigua and also when I moved to London. And into this mix came several foster children over the years.

But at a different point on the spectrum ...

Louise recalls ... Mine was largely a 'closed' family – a pale, watery shade of colour on my palette. Most of the time in our house, there was only my parents and my three siblings. Occasionally a family relative might plan to visit. I recall that usually they did not stay to eat a meal, but just had a drink and talked in the front room. Cousins might come with them sometimes and we would play together, but only downstairs.

Hearing Les talk about his family, and the fun and richness of relationships in having extended family involved in their lives as children, always made me wish that I had had that experience in my family, but we never got there in the same way. And I never appreciated the impact of my closed family on my expectations and comfort levels outside of this norm. In fact, for a few years after we were married, I would clench my teeth when Les said to someone – friend or family – 'Come on over!' I never felt it was quite right to be so spontaneous, inviting and open. There were times at Les's family gatherings when I felt a bit overwhelmed by his family. I now understand why!

We invite you as a couple to consider the shades of colour in each of the family culture types below. Some of this thinking may help to explain your feelings about each other's families and give you some insight as to the way forward in creating family relationships that work well for you as a couple but also encourages your wider families.

Position yourself somewhere on this spectrum, in between these extremes:

Closed family	*Open family*
immediate family only	wider extended family and others embraced
Being – only involved if asked	*Doing* – expecting to get involved and contribute
Planned – family involvement largely pre-arranged	*Spontaneous* – short notice required, ready to be involved

Lack of communication with wider family	*Lots of communication* with wider family
Relating to a select *few*	*All* invited mostly
Hierarchy – family deferring to, and gathering around, seniors	*Equality* – family led by whoever has a good idea

Family culture is important for fostering a strong sense of identity, community and purpose for family members. It is therefore important to appreciate the features of the family you have come from and the family you are joining with, especially in terms of how they do relationships.

What family relationship norms do you want drawn on your canvas? Something similar to what one or both of you have experienced, or something different? Your expectations of the behaviour you want to see in your own home need to be known and managed. Family members need to know what your expectations are as a couple. This will encourage clarity and harmony between you both.

Robert and Barbara were from different nationalities and had both lived in the UK for a few years. During their courtship, they realised very quickly that some of their cultural norms and background experiences were very similar. Most importantly, to them, they shared an appreciation of the same attitudes, values and behaviours, especially to do with the importance of family.

They were both quite excited about how they would want to do 'family' in terms of their own children and how they would encourage relationships with the wider family. This openness had been their experience, in both families, in the past. Robert and Barbara had clearly done some thinking and talking about what they wanted their marriage to look like culturally.

A few months after they were married, Barbara spoke sheepishly about a 'family' situation that she felt was 'a bit over the top'. A few of Robert's wider family had visited their new home and two of the female relatives had searched her kitchen thoroughly and helped themselves to whatever they wanted from the cupboards. Apparently they felt they could do this because they were family! Barbara was very uncomfortable with this and found it overwhelming. She didn't tell Robert how she felt.

Discussions about what is working and what makes either of you feel uncomfortable are valid – even after you have both agreed on your approach to these matters. It is normal (and recommended) that you revisit these conversations whenever you need to. This is simply a way of adjusting your position as you stand before the canvas and of acknowledging that sometimes the paint on the brush can look different, in colour and attractiveness, when it is actually applied to the canvas.

When they got engaged, it was easy for Aidan to introduce Alice to all his family and for her to get to know them before the wedding, because his family were always having parties or gatherings of some sort. The set-up and the food arrangements were well known by everyone. The venue changed often, but the unspoken expectation remained the same for festivals, celebrations and even just 'catch-up' times: everyone would turn up and bring food or drink. There would be lots of talk and laughter until late. Aidan and Alice's wedding day was no exception.

Alice loved the warm and open sense of family and community that was not present in her own family, but a couple of years after they got married, Alice wanted Christmas alone at home, just the two of them. The request was initially met with silence. Aidan had never considered the possibility. When the subject was raised again, it became a heated discussion, with Alice referring to '*your* family' and '*always* having to attend' and '*never* being free to do things by ourselves'.

Odette and Matthew assumed that they were in the same place about the importance of family: both loved the diversity of the cultural experiences they were sharing together and learning from. But an issue of privacy and boundaries arose shortly after they married.

Matthew and Odette were arguing about Odette's objection to his sisters being free to go into their (marital) bedroom. Odette's argument was that any other room in their flat was fine – they were free to enter and use whatever they needed – but not their bedroom, family or not. It was their private space. For Matthew, however, the statement 'family is family' meant there were no restrictions on what family could do. He realised that Odette was in a slightly different place on the family spectrum.

The issues in these relationships are to do with family boundaries in one way or another. Each one of us has a cultural background in terms of family experience that puts us somewhere on the 'closed' to 'open' family spectrum and the 'being' and 'doing' spectrum.

We have seen friction where couples have made assumptions about family – agreeing to a family event without first discussing it or at least asking their spouse if they want to go. Letting a family member stay over can also be a challenge for someone from a 'closed' family background.

We have found that the closer a couple are on the spectrum, the fewer family-related issues arise. Where you have differences, try working through how you will do family together using these guide points:

- Do not make assumptions about each other's family members. Talk to each other to get any relevant back stories.
- Negotiate when an issue arises, but also identify some principles for dealing with family on that issue in the future.
- Agree boundaries on time and space, especially if one of you is not accustomed to lots of wider family interaction.
- Try to present a united front with both families.
- Check with your spouse before agreeing family commitments.

Friends

It is not OK for your friends to paint on your marriage canvas either. In some culture groups friendships are as important as family relationships. For some individuals, there is little distinction between the two, such that the first time this demarcation comes into focus is when a dating relationship starts to deepen and one partner points out their discomfort with the intrusiveness of friends during their time together.

When Carol and Theo met and started to date, it wasn't long before Carol noticed some cultural differences between the two of them. She very quickly realised that dating Theo meant including his friends! Often his friends would just turn up at venues where she thought they would be alone together, whether it was for a walk or a dinner date.

Initially, this was fine and even fun. However, as the relationship progressed, Carol felt she needed to address this cultural expectation and difference. They finally agreed on the importance of communicating explicitly to each other and to friends their expectations and boundaries, in order to maintain friendships but also to allow their relationship as a couple to progress without conflict in this area.

We hope this illustration will encourage you to broach the topic of close friendships and their place in your partnership before and after marriage. It is a vital conversation that is sometimes not had because friends often have a history with your partner that is far longer than your relationship with them, so it is difficult to address this without seeming possessive or insensitive.

Uncovering roots of cultural sensitivity or insensitivity

Asking the question 'Where is that coming from?' suggests that you are ready to search for the root cause, the unconscious element, of a behaviour that has grown from the learned cultural norms of one partner during their earlier years. The question encourages you as a couple to be more reflective and less argumentative when issues come up, and especially when those issues recur or become inflammatory.

Some background cultural norms do not become evident until there is a trigger experience. Consider the story below, in which the trigger was the change to married status.

Catherine had no idea that her boyfriend Carl would become so prudish and controlling about her dress sense after they were married. He used to like the way she dressed and often complimented her. But in the first few months of married life, he started to suggest she change an item of clothing when they were going out, especially to see his family. What Catherine wore was obviously beginning to make Carl feel uncomfortable and it made Catherine feel frustrated and sad that he had become critical of the way she dressed.

Carl's change of preference was to do with notions of modesty that he had learned as a young person. When Catherine had been his girlfriend then fiancée, her style of dress was fine, but he felt differently about the same dress sense in her new status as a 'married woman'. He felt embarrassed, especially when they were with his family, but didn't know how to tell Catherine.

We have all learned norms from our families, often through the choices our parents made and the exposure that, as children, we had to certain rituals and life events.

For us, asking each other the question 'Where is that coming from?' has been important, as it has drawn out a cultural learning experience or, even more importantly at times, a lack of that experience. This can help explain attitudes and behaviour that seem insensitive, uncaring or strange, particularly around issues that are emotionally loaded and 'should' matter. These could have cultural roots.

You might be able to think of something right now that causes contention or frustration, and perhaps deserves another look. We encourage you to talk about this so that you can identify the cultural colours that underlie the situation.

Relationships with family and friends are always a work in progress. Sometimes it takes hard work to make progress! Nonetheless, it is important that in the midst of this you don't burn bridges. Stepping back and 'radio silence' are preferable to being regarded as the cause of a family fall-out. Your cultural differentness may be alluded to as part of the issue – such scapegoating is almost inevitable. Always try to aim for peace with your spouse's family, because they *are* family.

4
The colours of expectation

Your paint palette contains colours that have silently made their way into your life. We have covered the first significant group of these in Chapter 3, in relation to the colours that you inherit from your family. In this chapter, we will explore how the expectations that have been attached to your social position, family position and gender are also colours that you should recognise for their influence on you and their potential to shape your marriage in both positive and negative ways.

When you hear the word 'role', what do you think of? Many people will think of actors taking on a persona and performing it in a way that appears believable. In sociological terms, however, a role is the behaviour expected of an individual in a particular social position, such as father or daughter.

Culture provides the learned content of social roles. A role carries with it a comprehensive set of behaviours that are expected and socially recognised within a community or society. These are behaviours that provide for self and others a means of identifying and placing an individual in a society. Consequently, roles attract expectations to do with the fulfilment of duties within the family and the community. This is especially true of traditional non-Western societies.

Our expectations are informed by our deep culture. These are expectations that others have of us and the expectations we have of others. When everyone in a community has learned the same cultural norms, they come to expect certain behaviours, attitudes and responses from each other. Expectation is the anticipation of a response based on what a person knows or assumes they know.

We share knowledge about cultural norms and how they should be acted out in the community.

Where expectations are not met and there is a void, the response can be one of disappointment or a sense of confusion about what is missing. Where expectations are met with something other than what the cultural norm dictates, there can likewise be challenges or frustration for the individual who is anticipating a 'correct' response but gets something different.

Early in your marriage there is the potential for a period of turmoil related to expectations. It is most likely to occur during the first months and years of marriage. As a couple, think and talk about your expectations of each other, especially in your roles as husband and wife. Are there things that you may subconsciously expect when your partner becomes your spouse? Is there buried disappointment or frustration affecting how you do life together that surfaces when unrelated conflict situations arise?

Expectations are often culturally formed

Louise recalls ... My dad had very strong gender role ideas. He had come from a background of male family leadership and he prided himself on being a good father and an excellent DIY man around the home, with skills he learned 'back home' in the Caribbean. He was keen to teach my younger brother his DIY skills but not his daughters. (I didn't know how to change a lightbulb until I went to university, where a young female friend showed me how to do it!)

When my mother asked my dad to do a job around the house, it would usually be done before the close of day. At the very latest, by the end of the week. That background experience informed my unspoken expectations of Les when we were first married.

We bought our first house during our first year of married life. It was in a state of disrepair, but was 'a structurally solid little house', as Les said. So we moved in with the plan to do it up, bit by bit. This was when I first experienced extreme frustration with Les. I would ask him to help with various small DIY tasks, like putting up a curtain rail or picture hooks, but the tasks remained undone. I gave him time and asked again, but to no avail. My expectations of Les were based on my experience and observations of my father.

Les and I eventually talked about my expectations and his apparent lack of response. We laid out our very different upbringing experiences and eventually came to a solution that satisfied us both, which included the help of gifted friends and a good directory of tradespeople!

Where expectations are not met, it can result in a void, or in the feeling that something expected is missing or something *un*expected has happened instead. All of these scenarios have the potential to cause upset or frustration unless they are talked through and resolved.

Areas where expectations can be strong

Expectations about money – spending and saving – are often influenced by the example and explicit teaching of parents, or the lack of it.

Les recalls ... my mother reminded me often of the importance of saving money. Her instruction was always to try to save at least half of what you earn. This principle has stood me and my siblings in good stead financially over the years.

Finance is such an important area to plan and 'paint' together well, using complementary brush strokes. Talk about your spending and saving habits, your plans and ideas. Having differing unspoken expectations in relation to your finances can result in major contention and, potentially, can lead you into financial difficulty. Ask yourselves to what extent you have a shared vision for your finances. Consider who has the strongest financial management skills and use those strengths and disciplines to build and plan your financial goals together.

Take some time also to reflect on other expectations that have strong cultural roots for you. It is well worth scrutinising these and discussing what they looked like in your upbringing. Examples could be:

- contact and closeness with family
- childcare
- the gender-specific role of parents, at home or in the workplace
- diet
- celebrations
- friendships.

Role conflict

In adulthood, our individual roles are many and varied. Some are culturally dictated, others are not. We usually manage and juggle them well in our relationships with family, in the workplace, in church and in our marriage too. But when a role becomes complicated, this can produce an unexpected colour that is unplanned and imposed. When this unexpected colour is splashed on some part of our marriage canvas, it can create role conflict, often resulting in a change to the original, intended colour that is disconcerting. In other words, the expectation imposes a compromise or challenge in some way to our role as a marriage partner.

Taking on a new role, as we do when we become a husband or wife, can bring with it the feeling of being caught between the expectations of marital roles imagined (or enforced) by other people and our own expression of the actual role we want to have in our relationship. The conflict arises when we know that we must choose to please either those who have a historic familial influence on us or our partner, with whom we have agreed the actual roles we want to express in our home. Being genuinely unable to please both can be very stressful and anxiety-inducing, particularly early on in marriage, and might leave both partners feeling conflicted. The conflict arises from trying to satisfy those people who have expectations of us in each role but knowing that by satisfying one we may offend or dissatisfy the other.

As an example, imagine that a husband and wife have built their relationship around gender equity and shared roles in the home. When the husband's family visits, they expect him to leave all the work of preparing a meal to his wife. The role they expect him to have, and indeed the one he always used to have before he established a new role as husband, is based on male superiority. When he starts to help his wife prepare food, he is ridiculed by his parents, and his siblings tease him, saying loudly that he is 'under the thumb'. He knows that if he chooses to listen to his family, his wife will feel that he has ignored the new culture they have agreed on in their home and prioritised the role and behaviour that his parents chose.

Conflict like this can quickly escalate into a primal test of loyalty, in which you feel trapped, caught between different roles and unable to keep all parties happy.

Role conflict may surface wherever one of you feels that there are valid role expectations of you (from outside your marriage) that challenge your role inside the marriage and your commitment to it, especially where the expectations pre-existed your marriage. Being a father or mother to children who were born before you married is another common area that can bring you into conflict with role expectations that were established before your marriage. These conflicts may come to the surface as you do the kind of deliberate discussion and evaluation work on the colours of your marriage that we are recommending in this book.

It's quite possible that you are aware of tension or problems that sound exactly like this, but you have not yet put a name to them. Essentially, we are talking about the consequences of being pulled in different directions by the loved ones you each care about. In your background culture role, the expectations for you were clear, but now you might be starting to find that you have to negotiate a new role that challenges your background culture.

Practical issues can also cause role conflict, such as the constraints of time or money. Perhaps your family expect you to make some financial provision for them – and you always did when you were single. Now that you have a partner and family of your own, you may not have the ability (or the support of your spouse) to continue to meet the needs of those who look to you.

Hannah loved the involvement of Rohan's family with their wedding. Everything was special and no expense was spared by his parents, because he was the first-born son. At this stage, Hannah knew nothing of the responsibilities and expectations within the immediate and wider family, and the weighty role expectations that went with the role of 'first-born'. Rohan had not told her.

As time went by, Rohan felt conflicted but did not know how to begin a conversation with Hannah. His ageing parents had chosen to return 'home' and this meant that as first-born son Rohan held significant status as the first of three siblings.

Hannah and Rohan were saving to buy their first house when he was informed about a large medical expense that his parents needed help with. They had not asked Rohan, but an aunt had told him of their issue. No doubt the rest of the family knew and expected him to respond because he was the eldest son. Rohan's dilemma rested on the fact that he didn't think Hannah would take too kindly to a diversion of their house-buying funds to his parents. He thought she would question his loyalty to their young family and their financial goals.

Finally, and with help, Rohan realised that the issue was to do with cultural role expectations of the first-born. It was something he should have taken the time to talk about with Hannah at the start of their marriage. He owed it to her to let her know what she would be signing up to culturally – the good bits and the more challenging bits. But Rohan also realised that it was better to talk about it 'late' rather than 'never'. Nothing would undermine their relationship more than to syphon off money from their joint funds to help his parents without Hannah knowing and agreeing to it. That would severely compromise the trust between them. Rohan therefore broached the subject with Hannah.

Hannah was surprised by the whole story, especially the cultural role expectation bit. As a Christian, she believed in the kingdom principle of generosity. Generosity, she reasoned, sometimes involved personal sacrifice. This mindset enabled her to agree that, as a couple, they would help Rohan's parents. Hannah talked sympathetically with Rohan about how they could help financially and even encouraged her husband to spend a short time with them – a trip that was paid for out of their savings. Rohan's siblings also helped financially.

Rohan had to learn that he didn't have an obligation to his parents above his loyalty to his wife. It was not an either/or situation. But there was a life-long blessing to be had through honouring parents with support and encouragement.

Role-conflict situations may arise for you in different ways because of your background cultural differences. Unspoken expectations and a personal sense of pressure to meet those expectations is real role-conflict stress.

Identifying and naming the cultural origins of a problem and sharing those with your spouse is a good first step to unpacking the issues involved. Together, look at ways to resolve the problem and thereby ease any sense of awkwardness and anxiety that goes with a lack of honesty and openness in a close relationship. You might find that if the cultural nuances in your background that are causing anxiety are shared with your spouse, a problem shared is a problem halved. Some level of appreciation and support is most likely to be forthcoming.

Take some time now to reflect on any conflict you are experiencing that is generated by differing expectations of your role.

Expectations related to being the first-born

It may be useful for you to know how family expectations of the first-born offspring work. In many cultures, there are expectations related to being the first-born son, but for some it's the first-born daughter. These often relate to care-giving, finance and organising and leading family affairs, especially when parents are no longer able to do so due to ill-health or death. The onus is on that first-born offspring to rally the other siblings and take on the lion's share of support and leadership of the family.

These expectations are important to be aware of, especially where intercultural marriage includes a spouse from a Western society or background where this is unfamiliar. Appreciating the gravity of this expectation in a way that means one spouse can support and encourage the other in this role is a special grace in the marriage.

Where one spouse has to constantly plead for and justify their need to fulfil family expectations and obligations, this can put a strain on the relationship. When, however, their spouse appreciates the importance of honouring parents and the expectation to, at times, make sacrifices to do this, it is a challenge but ultimately also a blessing as the couple can together agree how expectations will be met within their means.

5
Unwanted colours

Cultural values and norms help to bind people together and keep them united. They are meant for the good of those in the society in which they are used, by providing, if you like, a template for doing life as families and communities to make it safe and promote consensus and harmony. Shared beliefs, norms and values – the deep-culture material – is meant for the benefit of all.

Unfortunately, however, some have suffered because of the impact of cultural norms and expectations. For those who don't conform (through no fault of their own), untold hurt and pain may be experienced.

So far you have reflected individually on your deep and surface culture – the things that make you *you*. We have encouraged you to begin to notice and deal with your likes and dislikes and the strength of your feelings – the depth of the colours on your paint palette. There is one final area that we invite you to reflect on and talk about together, and this is what we are calling 'ugly' and unwanted colours.

We define these as negative experiences that have their roots in learned cultural norms and responses that impact harshly on an individual's person, self-esteem and/or sense of identity. Ugly colours from *outside* are behaviours towards an ethnic or cultural group by those outside of that group. Racism is an example of this, along with prejudice and discrimination based on ethnicity.

In our multicultural society, where several cultures and ethnic groups live together, the mix is not always harmonious. Continuing the metaphor of the artist's palette, racism, prejudice and discrimination can be present as ugly colours. One spouse may experience this more than the other, in subtle or overt ways. Such experiences in the workplace and elsewhere can be particularly wearing and undermining. When they are suffered in public, this can be alarming and offensive. When they are directed against you as an intercultural couple it can be disconcerting.

Ugly colours created from outside your culture

Prejudice

Many of our prejudices are learned in much the same way as our cultural norms. In fact, they are often formed as a part of our cultural learning. Prejudices are negative preconceived ideas and opinions, often not based on actual experience.

We are saddened by the hypocrisy that we have seen in some parents. At the outset, when their son or daughter is just friends with a young person from another culture, they are very accepting of the friendship. However, when friendship turns to love and marriage, it's a different story. Suddenly, prejudice and negativity can become apparent.

Daniel and Mica had been engaged for three years. They had not yet married, because they were waiting for Daniel's mother to accept her son's choice of marriage partner and allow herself to get to know Mica. Daniel's father was much more accepting, but Mum was not shifting!

Daniel's mum made it clear to her son that by marrying this young woman, he would be 'marrying beneath them'. She regarded her family as superior and this young woman was not good enough.

Daniel and Mica had put their lives on hold for three years, but his mother's prejudice was not going away. They eventually decided they should trust God's leading, get married and get on with their lives (as their pastor had suggested). Three years later, they are happily married and now have a son, whom Daniel's mother has only chosen to see once.

Racism

For some of us, our cultural identity is all the more profound because of our experience of racism. Many have experienced discrimination as thick or thin brush strokes throughout life, but have overcome it and moved on. That's great if you have been able to do it, but if not, this moment at which you stand together as a couple at the point of marriage might be the right time to find healing before you move forward. Acknowledging and addressing racism and prejudice as a couple could be healing and strengthening. As someone once said, hurting people hurt people. Importantly, therefore, you can choose to work together through the ways in which you might manage these ugly colours and their impact on yourselves and your future family.

Knowing that your spouse is experiencing discrimination can be truly painful. Empathy and ongoing support are so important for getting through the experience while maintaining good mental health. Unfortunately, experiences of racism, prejudice and discrimination may happen again in a different place, time or guise. Evaluating and learning from these together can strengthen your relationship as a couple.

There are many racism awareness courses available, which help employers, employees and others appreciate the issues around racism and its impact on individuals and groups. Attending such a course together could help you or your spouse appreciate more fully the lived experience of racism in the other person's life. Most importantly, it will better enable you to support each other appropriately in terms of strategies and responses.

It is also possible that one or both of you is living in the shadow of horror stories about mixed-culture marriages. These can be inherited or 'fresh'. One or both of you may have had to listen to a variety of voices and opinions on your relationship (see Chapter 3).

Ultimately, we want you to consider how big these issues are for you at this time and how they form part of your personal colour palette. Take some time to reflect individually on the questions below and then, when you are ready, share your experiences with each other.

- Has either of you been the victim of racism or discrimination? What happened? Jot down the key points.
- Have you already shared the hurtful details with your partner?
- If you haven't, what stopped you from telling your partner?
- How would you like your partner to support you when dealing with such experiences in the future?
- How might you support each other if you have to deal with prejudice from outsiders towards you as an intercultural couple?

Ugly colours created from within your culture

This is learned behaviour taught by those *within* a culture group towards those in the group. It has the impact of hurting or penalising those who are judged to have failed in measuring up to what is culturally applauded. One example is notions of beauty. Judgements about what is *not* beautiful can be emotionally painful and damaging to an individual's self-esteem. We mention this here, along with other examples, because as a couple one of you may have been the victim of such behaviour and may inadvertently carry the impact of it into your marriage.

Rebecca had grown up believing she was not pretty because of her nose. In some cultures, the more pointed and straight your nose is, the fairer you are considered to be. This cultural notion of beauty fuelled relentless teasing and ridicule throughout Rebecca's childhood, even from family members. When Rebecca married, she and Bradley worked together to create very bright new colours to replace those she had experienced. The past could not be undone, but Bradley's sensitivity and affirmation took Rebecca to a better place of self-love.

Intentional brush strokes can brighten or lighten deep-culture experiences, but they cannot fully eliminate them. We say this, because many of these have deep roots in our personal identity. You may, for example, disown and refuse to carry certain cultural views forward into your marriage, but nonetheless they have played a part in forming you as a person. This cannot be completely erased, but it can instead be managed, for example, to build resilience or to create a counter, more positive, self-narrative.

Some ugly colours appear in all cultures. Here are a few examples:

Female circumcision (female genital mutilation)

This is still practised in some cultures in the belief that it maintains sexual purity in women. This experience as a child will continue to affect adult women, physically and emotionally. It can also have a negative impact on sexual intimacy in marriage.

Severe pressure to achieve academically

If someone comes from a family where most others are academically able and they are not, their experience of verbal abuse and put-downs may have created a sense of inferiority in them.

The stigma of mental or physical disability

In some cultures, particularly Asian and South American, there is shame associated with any evident disability. It comes from a belief that the impairment has been caused by the individual or a family member doing something wrong, or by evil magic or an ancestral curse. This can lead the family to deny that the child has a disability (and therefore not get help for it) or to hide the child away.

Being the recipient of such lifelong negative reactions is a 'colouring' that can be lovingly redressed together and, if necessary, with professional help.

Gender stereotypes and sexism

The superiority and value of boys over girls and men over women is a norm in some cultures.

> Lorraine described how, 'back home', being a family of girls with no brothers was hard. The family was treated differently – looked down upon. In her culture, boys improved the family's status. She often had a hard time at school for this reason. Lorraine knew that this had affected her sense of self-worth for many years.
>
> She didn't really appreciate how much this had affected her until she got married and had a daughter. She shared her experience with her husband and together they prayed and determined that their girls would have a much more positive life experience than she had had. They made new colours!

The negative experience came back to Lorraine when she knew that God wanted her to lead a particular ministry. She wrestled with her lack of self-worth, not fully realising where it came from and how profound it was. Her husband discerned the link with the derogatory words and experiences she had endured as a girl growing up. Together they were able to pray and ask God to undo the negativity and ugliness of her childhood experience.

Cultural stereotypes about masculinity are learned and can impact emotional intimacy in your marriage.

Derek had learned not to talk about his feelings. From an early age he was discouraged from this and instructed instead to 'man up'. He was also regularly told, 'Don't be a baby', 'Keep it moving', 'Don't be emotional'. When he married, he found that his wife wanted him to talk with her about his feelings and emotions, and she wasn't able to appreciate why he found this so difficult.

Being called a tomboy is not nice for a girl, especially if it is used as a slur or to compare her negatively to female siblings. It is a label that says you are not feminine in your demeanour or appearance compared with other girls. It can be the first rung on the ladder of low self-esteem for some young women.

Sexism in a culture can cause men to perceive and treat women in ways that keep them from thriving and encourage them to have limited expectations of themselves. This can happen even when they have moved out of their cultural context, because the norms and the pressure are great.

Glen, a wise father, opened a discussion with his future son-in-law before he agreed to the marriage of his daughter.

'I know you love her and she loves you,' he said, 'but I need to know more about the family she is marrying into. I know that your cultural background is very patriarchal and men are regarded as superior to women. Generally, women are expected to be subservient to men and not encouraged to be independent or ambitious, financially or academically. My daughter has told me that you are not like that, even though you lived in your home country until you were a teenager. Nonetheless, families can put pressure on their sons to bring their wives in line. Young man,' he continued, 'how will my daughter, in whom I have invested so much, get on in your family?'

Glen knew what he was talking about and had seen numerous examples of sexism in other mixed-culture marriages. He was saddened by the family pressure that ultimately frustrated and undermined good, able young women – women who had not been allowed to pursue their chosen career or invest in continuous professional development because their husbands had been 'cautioned' by other men in the family.

This was a wake-up call for the young man. He was now forewarned and forearmed to be vigilant about matters concerning his new wife and the possibility of peer and family pressure, which he had given very little thought to in the past. In due course, the couple married and both went on to thrive and develop in every sphere of their life together, largely because of Glen's intentional interventions.

Glen had articulated his concerns, identifying the cultural components of his future son-in-law's background and upbringing that could potentially impact the wellbeing of his daughter. It was cultural behaviour which, he knew, continued to be played out in women's lives today. His discussion with his future son-in-law made the young man conscious of those around him – family and church friends – whose words and actions could damage the gender equality that he and his future wife were committed to. It encouraged him to be proactive in listening for and warding off those voices and attitudes that so concerned his father-in-law and himself.

Not everyone wants to talk openly and rationally, even if they can articulate the issues that concern them about your marriage to someone from a different culture. But we recommend giving the people whose opinion you value the opportunity to talk out their concerns and objections; they may provide insights you have not considered. There are some good learning points to be gleaned from the experiences of others. Take some time to reflect on what you have observed or experienced personally or socially in your culture that makes you uncomfortable because of its impact at some point in your past? Will it impact your future together if you do not proactively address it? Will it put pressure on you to behave in certain ways?

Learned behaviour

Racism, prejudice and discrimination are all learned responses. They are behaviours that we can go on to repeat and to teach in our own families (even though we have been the victim of such behaviour) unless we consciously exclude them. It is all too easy and likely that what we have seen as we grow up will be what we perpetuate in our own relationships and household.

Jude described how he was brought up in a home where shouting was the norm. He realised, as he sat in our marriage preparation session and listened to other couples talk, that this was not healthy. He had been ready to imitate this verbal aggression in his own relationship and embark on married life with an instinctive reflex to shout at his fiancée about the smallest of things. This was now not what he wanted in his marriage.

We learn behaviour by watching it. Often what we see is what we do, with little consideration for its impact. We encourage you to be aware of all that you are bringing into your marriage. When we subconsciously copy behaviours and attitudes, these things can set the tone in our homes. We allow things onto our own artist's palette and from there, without noticing, we paint them straight onto our marriage canvas. Our hope is that this book will prompt you to look at these things and the effect they have – personal, familial and cultural – so that you don't allow anything into your marriage without evaluating its potential impact.

We know that prejudice and intolerance exist, even among Christian families, so we must consider how these have impacted us. We must also begin to examine ourselves and ask, 'What are our own cultural prejudices?' If our son or daughter were to decide to marry, would we be sufficiently content with them choosing a person of good character, regardless of their ethnic or cultural background? For Christian readers, should their faith be taken into consideration?

The place of forgiveness

Choosing a spouse who does not conform to the expectations of family because they are from an 'unaccepted' ethnic group can result in feelings of rejection, and this is experienced by each partner in a different way. For one it may be pain caused by others remonstrating with them and refusing to accept their choice.

For the other, the pain is caused by rejection and the feeling that they are not accepted because they are not good enough! Both experiences are very hurtful. They become even more challenging when the couple go ahead and marry and, thereafter, they must continue to interact with those who blatantly expressed their rejection. Words spoken and attitudes that convey rejection remain painfully alive in the mind and emotions, and can affect future interactions with in-laws, family members and church members as unforgiveness and bitterness take root.

As Christians we believe that forgiveness has a spiritual dimension. We believe that the forgiveness of Christ saves, and that unforgiveness creates and sustains tension and division in your relationship as a couple. The pervasiveness of unforgiveness can also affect you as individuals in your relationships with other people. Unforgiveness can plague families and church communities. It can be the root cause of animosity and distance between members for years, even generations. Suffice it to say, unforgiveness is emotionally cancerous.

John and Karen wanted to marry. As a Christian couple, they believed this was God's plan for them. Karen's parents had no objections – they knew John and his parents well. John's mother, however, had strong objections and found it hard to accept the possibility of marriage between her first-born son and a woman from a different cultural background. She encouraged family members to speak to the couple to dissuade them from marrying. People in the church (including elders) were encouraged by John's mother to tell them, in no uncertain terms, that their union would not be compatible because, as the first-born son, John should have a wife from their cultural background. Not Karen.

John and Karen deferred the marriage by more than two years to get John's mum on side, but to no avail. Finally, John's father stepped in and spoke to Karen's father, approving the marriage.

The couple spoke repeatedly of their desire to honour their parents, saying, 'That is what we were taught as Christians. It's an important commandment in the Bible.' They knew the scripture that endorsed this position in their minds.

They listened and waited and prayed in the midst of the opposition.

When, finally, John and Karen were married, John's mother accepted the marriage. Karen observed that, strangely, her mother-in-law behaved as if nothing untoward had transpired between them over the past few years! No apology was forthcoming.

Karen's challenge was to forgive her mother-in-law, and others, for the venomous and hurtful comments that had been levelled at her to try to keep her apart from John.

The questions you are left with at the end of any struggle or conflict related to your intercultural marriage are: 'What should our response be, going forward?' and 'How can we protect our emotional and spiritual health?'

Acknowledge and talk together about the pain of the experience you have been forced to face. The pain will be slightly different for each of you. It is important to appreciate that your spouse is not blaming you by proxy, so there is no need for defensiveness. Listen to and acknowledge what they are saying and have felt. Consider confiding in a trusted person like a church leader, or another couple, who can help you by listening and by praying for you. Subsequently, if you feel you need to move away from a particular setting, or even if you decide to remain, you will be taking the first steps to setting yourself free to move forward in your marriage without looking back with hurt. Be prayerful and unhurried about any decision to move on. As Christians it is important to know God's leading when you make such a decision.

Choose to forgive everything: words, actions and incidents. This will release you from the people and experiences that have hurt you so that you can heal and move on completely. The people you need to forgive may still be entrenched in their opinion and opposition; you cannot change them, but you can help yourself and keep your marriage from being affected by roots of bitterness in the future.

Forgiveness is a kingdom-culture value which, in our example above, Karen knew she had to embrace for her own spiritual progress and emotional health. Karen wanted to forgive from the heart, so she first needed to be honest with God and herself regarding how she felt about that episode in her life and the people involved. Then, humbly, she let go of the offence and released forgiveness, particularly towards her mother-in-law, even though there has, to date, never been an apology from her.

Forgiveness is encouraged in the Bible, but it is not something that happens lightly. It requires us to let go of hurt and offence and to choose to live free from bitterness and, if possible, peaceably with those who have made it clear that they do not accept us.

Forgiveness, for you, may need to be a colour you choose to paint over past personal cultural experiences that have impacted you negatively. This is the kingdom value that best deals with the ugly colours showing through from your cultural background and continuing to negatively affect your life and self-esteem today.

If unforgiveness linked to your background culture continues to be an issue for you or your spouse, we suggest you start with our 'Further reading' section at the back of this book and dig a bit deeper into this topic. You might also want to find counselling support to free yourself from the bondage of unforgiveness and any bitterness that needs uprooting. These are ugly colours that you do not need on your colour palette or indeed on your marriage canvas.

Time to reflect

This chapter has contained some examples to illustrate areas of life where culturally 'ugly' colours can appear. Hopefully they have been enough to remind you about your personal experiences, possibly related to the impact of other social behaviours, yet with what you now know to be cultural roots.

Take the time to think about and share together any unpleasant cultural experiences or learned behaviours. Be aware that these may have been repressed because they are so painful. Remind yourself that you are engaging with these unpleasant memories because they may have a negative effect on how you do life as a couple. You are recognising that they may appear on your artist's palette.

Use the image on page 161 to annotate with any new colours you have become aware of.

6

Your cultural profile

As you begin this exploration of your relationship, the ideal is for both of you to have an equal say about what your cultural colours will look like, together, on the canvas. It is good to encourage each other by letting your spouse know that you value what they bring to the marriage and that you want to know more about the currently unknown parts of their cultural background. The aim is to see in each other everything that has the potential to be painted onto the marriage canvas and contribute to the artwork. Showing your true colours and working together to identify what to use, change or discard is vitally important for the health of your marriage. These intentional conversations will create understanding and intimacy between you as a couple. To know and be known is foundational for the sort of friendship that a thriving and healthy marriage must be based on.

Stand an equal distance from the canvas

We illustrate this with the image of two people standing before a canvas on which they are going to paint. Both of them need to have equal access to the canvas and be able to see it from the same angle. In marriage it is so important to feel that your opinions, concerns and ideals are valued by your spouse. You might assume that this is a given at the point of getting married, but without being intentional, familiarity can block out times of dialogue and listening carefully to each other.

It is very easy for the most vociferous and forthright partner to dominate the canvas and painting. But painting the background and the foreground, and the types of brush strokes that will be used, needs to be a shared artistic process, with both of you consciously contributing. That is not to say that a marriage can't look more like the culture of one spouse than the other. The key point is that, together, you have agreed the emphasis with careful regard for each other.

> *Louise recalls ... We had dinner with a couple and their children, and unintentionally caused a brief spat at the dining table when Les asked the children about a food from the mother's cultural background, to which they responded, 'What's that?'*
>
> *Edith, their mother, replied, 'They don't know it and they won't like it either, because their father always turns his nose up at most of my traditional meals, so the children see that and copy him!'*

Cultural colours need to be endorsed by both of you in the home. Personal preference, as in the case of food, should not necessarily disallow a cultural experience that is valued by one spouse. The task is to look at its importance and how it can be assimilated in an affirming way. Intercultural marriage, done well, requires an acknowledgement of differentness and an appreciation of this as a starting point for dialogue and fusion.

Two brushes on one canvas

'Do two walk together unless they have agreed to do so?' This is a question asked by the prophet Amos in the Old Testament (Amos 3:3). Just like Amos, we are asking: can two work together or produce a good outcome unless they agree on the purpose and process? Standing together, each with a different clutch of cultural norms, each on a continuum from similar to different, is not enough. The ground on which you stand must have the same foundations of friendship, love, trust, forgiveness and commitment.

The solid foundation stones in your marriage relationship undergird the building and crafting of it. Your perspectives of culture will surface at times to cause challenges or frustrations as you progress in your marriage. If, however, you are both standing on the same foundations and are able to maintain your position (nurturing these qualities in your marriage), the canvas painting and artwork outcomes will be a picture of well-blended colours. The deliberate accents of colour that are uniquely yours will become apparent in your marriage union and will be appreciated, not just tolerated.

Take the opportunity to reflect on your own cultural profile. Set aside some time to do this thoughtfully and independently before sharing it with your fiancé or spouse.

The paint brush

Every painter has a brush. This represents the conscious and subconscious behaviours and attitudes that you use to perpetuate or alter learned cultural norms and determine which of them you will take into your partnership. Brush strokes can carry colour from your own palette or canvas to your marriage canvas. The brush is your conscious or subconscious will, taking and applying colours from the palette, strongly or lightly, into your married life together.

However, the strength of the brush stroke will determine what that colour will ultimately look like on the canvas.

Vicky was born in the UK but was brought up steeped in the West African cultural traditions of her family. She knew the language, greetings, expectations, values and so on. These were strong cultural colours. When she fell in love with Vernon, a young Scottish man, they talked for hours about what their marriage would look like culturally. Vicky intentionally toned down her vibrant cultural brush strokes, as did Vernon, to honour and value each other's cultural identity.

They began instead to paint a somewhat eclectic but mutually satisfying picture in the first season of their marriage. In terms of the food they cooked, Vicky toned down her highly spiced food by eliminating chilli peppers from their diet on most days, even though it was an ingredient she usually enjoyed from her West African cultural background. Instead, they together adopted their own multicultural variety of regular dishes. On Fridays, however, they had an 'anything goes' policy!

The couple chose to tone up Vicky's language, using stronger brush strokes, by beginning to teach Vernon some greetings and phrases to help him in family situations. Vernon toned down his very frequent visits to family in Scotland (at least until the children were born). Together they agreed what they thought was best for them at the start of their marriage.

What is on your personal palette?

We have now reached the point where you begin to reflect on your own cultural colours and create a cultural profile. We invite you to answer the questions attached as you go through each section. At the end of this chapter you will find a QR code that you can use to download a paint palette. This can be edited to reflect your profile, and will be a tool for leading and informing your discussions. Share it with your partner!

Deep culture

First, we invite you to think about your own origins and upbringing. What resonates with you in terms of recollections of your early years?

Notice which words in the word cloud below stand out for you as a cultural trait, either in your surface culture or in your deep culture. Can you illustrate this from your life experience with more than one example? This will give you some indication of its importance as a cultural trait endorsed by your background culture.

For example, we would both circle 'gender roles', because we each had strong and obvious gender examples endorsed regularly from an early age.

Louise recalls ... I used to love hearing my dad whistling a tune as he came in from shift work in the early morning. At the age of nine, I remember how comforting it was to hear his keys jangle in the door just as he finished the tune he was whistling. One day, I chose to whistle a tune that was in my head. My dad promptly told me to stop whistling. He was obviously annoyed with me. As he left the room, my mother came in and said in a matter-of-fact way, 'Girls don't whistle. A whistling woman and a crowing hen are good for neither God nor men!'

Les recalls ... The story Louise shared earlier about my pay packet is an example of strong gender-role expectations. Another example was my mum's insistence on making sure that each of her three sons, including myself, could wash, cook and iron competently. This was for two reasons: first, so that we could look after ourselves well if we stayed single and, second, so that we could manage well if we married what she called a 'worthless woman' – one who didn't know how to do 'women's' household tasks well!

In the word cloud below, we have tried to create a comprehensive list of deep-culture characteristics. Feel free to ignore whatever does not apply to you and add anything that is missing.

Your cultural profile

housing
personal space
success morality money
extended family beauty
the elderly manners courtship
religion values modesty body language
ageing ambition touch work privacy
customs
rituals traditions eye contact
family cleanliness
child-rearing hospitality beliefs
humour gender roles
emotion communication

Circle any words that you feel explain or illustrate your deep (inherited) culture. You might like to share with your partner or use it as the basis of your discussion.

The next step is to reflect on where these cultural traits have come from. Use the bullet points below to guide you. Which of your deep-culture elements have you inherited from

- your birth country?
- the country where you now live?
- your father's culture?
- your mother's culture?
- your friendship group?
- somewhere else?

Louise recalls ... Traditions and rituals around death and dying vary significantly in different cultures. In Caribbean and African cultures there are expectations about visits and providing gifts. I recall being criticised by a lady at church for not visiting her when her husband died, especially since I was the pastor's wife. However, I didn't appreciate the depth of the offence she felt for many years.

I had grown up in a household where, as children, we were never taken to funerals or the homes of bereaved families, even though we were a family of Caribbean heritage, where traditions and rituals to do with bereavement are prevalent and important.

In contrast, Les was often taken to funerals and visited bereaved families as a child, both here in the UK and in Antigua. He saw and experienced the tone and content of conversations, and the ways in which support was given to the bereaved. Consequently, he knows from experience how to respond appropriately to death and dying.

Asking each other the question 'Where does that come from?' is important, as it could draw out a cultural learning experience or, even more importantly at times, a lack of such experience, which could help explain current attitudes and behaviour. Behaviour that seems insensitive, uncaring or strange regarding things that 'should' matter could have cultural roots.

You may even be able to think of something right now that causes contention or frustration. This maybe deserves another look, to identify and talk about the cultural colours that underlie the situation.

Surface culture

Let's move on to think about the traditions and customs that are part of your cultural identity at a visible, surface level. Consider each of the areas below, and make some notes, feeling free to ignore those that do not apply to you or adding those that do.

- Food and cooking
- Hospitality

- Language
- Dress
- Music
- Holidays and leisure

The impact of diversity

We all, to some extent, have multicultural colours in our palette; those who are preparing for marriage need to realise this and evaluate them. The culture of the host society, alongside other cultural influences, affects our surface culture and can even impact our deep culture. It is good to identify in what ways this may be, for better or for worse, and make conscious choices. Many Muslims, for example, frown at what they regard as the immodest dress that women are allowed in British culture, and they are conscious about resisting it in their families.

As a global citizen, what are the multicultural experiences you have come to take for granted as your life has touched a variety of other cultures? Simply through working, socialising, shopping and so on, cultural differences become apparent, are accommodated, then assimilated by ourselves and others.

Louise recalls … When we moved from north London to south London, I would visit Brixton Market, enjoying walking through the stalls, looking and listening, especially to the haggling conversations between stall holders and shoppers. They drew me in, particularly because it was not a practice I had experienced when shopping in north London. There was no animosity in the haggling; it was just a loud, lively verbal exchange with accompanying expansive gestures, laughter and bravado until a price was finally settled upon, be it for meat, fabric, vegetables or whatever.

Haggling is a very common practice in the street markets of non-Western countries, where traders expect to be challenged on price. Haggling has become an expectation in Brixton, and other markets in south London, where people of non-Western cultures shop. During the first months of our life south of the river, we both learned to haggle. I am a lot better at it than Les and have brought home some real bargains!

Take some time to work through the questions below. These will guide you to think about how you are influenced by the cultures around you.

Exposure to a variety of people from different cultures presents opportunities for cultural learning that can endear you as a couple and your family to others. For example, giving and receiving cultural greetings that include correct gestures or in a native language, understanding the inappropriateness of the left hand, knowing when to give gifts, and many other cultural practices. These can help to smooth your transition into personal relationships.

Marcia was so pleased that David had given her the heads up about what gifts to take for each family member when she met her prospective in-laws for the first time. It made for a good start and a great first impression. She realised that if she'd been left to her own devices, she would have got it all wrong and made such inappropriate choices.

Consider the questions below and make some notes as you talk.

- What have you adopted from other cultures that is now part of your palette?
- What are some features of the surface culture in which you live now that are important to you?

- What do you do to accommodate the culture of the society/ community in which you now live?
- What do you do to maintain and nurture your deep-culture distinctiveness?
- The Bible encourages us to recall decrees, commands and regulations that translate into values, beliefs, traditions and experiences. It says to use and teach these things to honour God and enrich our lives (see Deuteronomy 4:1–9). From your Christian perspective, what, in the culture around you, do you allow and encourage, or reject? (We will develop this thinking later, in Chapter 8.)

When you appreciate multiculturalism as a couple, you become global citizens, better able to accept and adapt to differentness between and around you more naturally. We hope that you will now have a clearer idea of what is on your painting palette and you may have named some cultural elements that have become part of your identity but never been named before. Living as we do in culturally diverse settings, these are important questions to ask ourselves so that our artist's palette can fully express what we are bringing to our marriage.

What depth of colour are you using?

Depth of colour is our way of referring to how strongly or weakly you choose to emphasise a cultural norm and live it out in your marriage; for example, the level of connection you have as a couple with your extended family, or the extent to which you choose to embrace some of your religious cultural traditions, or whether you observe traditional dress codes at formal gatherings.

The paint

Each paint colour is one item of material (surface) or immaterial (deep) culture referred to by Edward T. Hall. These cultural norms have been learned since early childhood and therefore painted on your personal art canvas – they are your cultural life experience.

Metaphorically speaking however, as we have said before, the paint colours on your personal art canvas never dry completely. This is especially true for the foreground colours of surface culture. The background colours of deep culture will always leave some residual colour, even if erased (like a memory that has no emotion attached to it), but they can be painted over. In other words, learned cultural traits can be unlearned, adapted or strengthened to become lighter or brighter colours for you personally and on your shared married life canvas.

Finally, take a moment to summarise the key elements of your multicultural profile:

- What are your background colours?
- What is the depth of your background colours?
- What are your foreground colours?
- What is the depth of your foreground colours?

Using the image on page 161, find a moment when you are able to spend time with your partner and share your palettes with each other.

Part 3

PRINCIPLES FOR PAINTING TOGETHER

7
The picture frame

This book is about intercultural marriage, but the subject cannot be fully addressed, nor the issues dealt with, in a vacuum. The basic requirements for developing and nurturing your marriage relationship need to be in place. So, although this is not a general marriage advice book as such, we feel it is necessary to include some basics to encourage your marriage health – similar to those we would suggest to any married couple. We talk about this as the framework in which all discussions, differences and growth will take place. It's the foundation of your relationship. So, continuing with the artwork analogy, here we go.

The picture frame is an essential part of your marriage artwork, providing a surrounding boundary and context in which you 'do' marriage. However similar or dissimilar you are culturally, the framework of your married life needs to be nurtured and maintained. To use another analogy, the framework acts like a baby's cot bumper, which provides a soft and protective surrounding for the child. Even when crying and thrashing about, the child is in a safe place.

There are a few parts to the picture frame that we would suggest you consciously construct as a couple and maintain in your marriage repertoire, to form an encouraging and safe environment for sharing discussions, feelings, memories and concerns openly with your spouse, especially as an intercultural couple.

Parts of the picture frame

Friendship

Becoming friends by getting to know each other and developing fondness for each other is a vital step into a healthy marriage relationship. Many years down the line, it will be important to remind yourselves of how you met and the characteristics you appreciated most about each other when your friendship was first developing. We're not encouraging you to live in the past, or regret the changes that inevitably will take place, but rather to recall and celebrate the features of your relationship that made for a good, foundational friendship out of which love grew.

It is so easy to undermine this foundation stone of friendship in your marriage simply by neglecting it. Keeping friendship alive is fundamental to a healthy marriage. Many newly-weds describe themselves as having moved in with their best friend, but after a few years they are no longer best friends enjoying each other's company, because no effort is being made to nurture friendship. It is good to look back and try to re-establish some of the activities, actions and attitudes that kept the friendship alive, dynamic and full of pleasure. As the German philosopher Friedrich Nietzsche is thought to have said, 'It is not a lack of love, but a lack of friendship that makes an unhappy marriage.'

Loving care

Care is a subset of love. Loving care, demonstrated in both words and actions, means showing that you are deeply concerned about each other. It is important to be in tune with and use your spouse's 'love language' to connect with them often. Loving care is accumulated, so even when you are upset with each other, you can rest assured in your partner's genuine concern and appreciation. When we, as a couple, are out of sorts, we can sit in silence in each other's company and not feel uncomfortable, because fundamentally we have a stockpile of caring, respectful behaviours that have genuinely conveyed loving care in the past, such that they 'buffer' any current friction.

Take some time to reflect on what loving care looks like for each of you in your relationship.

Affirmation

This is another part of your picture frame. Affirmation is emotional support and encouragement in what you say and do, both to and for your spouse. This promotes a positive self-esteem in your partner, but also draws you closer together as you trust that any critiquing or suggestions will be for the other's betterment. We once heard someone say that he was the captain and cheerleader of his wife's fan club. To us, that is a good mindset for consciously affirming your partner.

Criticism and cynicism have the opposite effect to affirmation. They create a hard, harsh backdrop to a marriage relationship, such that partners will shut their hearts off from each other to protect themselves from emotional harm. Constant criticism tends to shut down intimate conversation.

Deep communication

Trust is built by mutual openness and honesty, and a willingness to share details about yourselves because neither of you has anything to hide from the other. Transparency in marriage is when there is no reticence about revealing who you are to your spouse. In an intercultural marriage, it is very much about revealing what has made you *you* and what is important in that information.

John Powell, author of *Why Am I Afraid to Tell You Who I Am?* (1999), suggests there are five levels of communication – each deeper, more engaging and more revealing of self than the one prior. Trust and transparency help to enable the transition to deeper levels of communication. This is what he says, in summary, about the five levels:

1. *Cliché conversation level* – This is the shallowest and least risky type of encounter; for example, 'Lovely weather today' or 'Please pass the sauce'. It's at a level that asks for unimportant information and requires only a limited response. A couple can exist in a perfunctory way with this and Level 2 communication. There is no openness beyond what is absolutely necessary.
2. *Reporting facts about others* – This level involves sharing information about what others have been doing or saying. These are observations without the addition of a value judgement that exposes our own feelings or thoughts about it; for example, 'The dustbins were not put out'.
3. *Sharing ideas or judgements* – This deeper level involves revealing some of our opinions. As we relate what we think, we test the waters carefully to be sure we are safe and will not get a negative reaction, a dismissal of our contribution as trite and unimportant, or a rebuff; for example, 'I like that brand of ...' or 'I think that ...'.
4. *Sharing feelings or emotions* – At this level we reveal ourselves, showing what lies behind our ideas and judgements; for example: 'I felt very happy when ... because ...'. This level of communication is achieved when we think our words and feelings will be heard, and encouragement to share more is likely to be forthcoming.
5. *Unguarded freedom to be completely honest* – The risk factor is no longer present, because we have learned to trust one another in our communication. We are therefore willing to share more fully, and at a deeper level, our dreams, hopes and vision – our deepest thoughts.

Each level of communication involves a deeper level of self-disclosure and intimacy and trust. But individuals do not get to the deeper levels often, without time, encouragement and a context conducive to sharing self.

Greg did a lot of the talking in his marriage to Gwen. Gwen, on the other hand, was a good listener. Their relationship, in Greg's words, had 'got stuck'. The source of the problem was communication. Gwen loved Greg very much, but being an introvert, she had become complacent and accustomed to not sharing with him beyond superficial conversation. Instead, she was quite happy with her inner conversations, especially since Greg usually and naturally filled up the 'talk space' in their home. Her mother was of a similar temperament and, Gwen knew, there was an added dynamic of the wider family cultural background of dominant men and more placid women. Greg and Gwen both wanted their relationship to grow closer, but didn't know how to make progress.

When asked about the levels of communication in their relationship, they soon spotted that there had been no real Level 4 or 5 communication since they had got married eighteen months previously. Greg the extrovert, without realising it, was not giving Gwen the encouragement or space to share her own valid feelings, ideas and thoughts. Gwen tended to 'own' Greg's views instead of thinking through and articulating her own. They were keen to explore the cause of the reticence, including its possible cultural roots. Greg and Gwen agreed to work on change, which included intentional 'Gwen talk time', usually when they went for a long walk. These times, Gwen said, were awkward at first, but with encouragement they became valuable, revealing and enhancing to their cultural relationship.

Submission and humility

Submission in marriage is about yielding to each other to accomplish goals that will ultimately benefit both of you. But it is also encouraging leadership where, in parts of the marriage, your spouse's skill outshines yours, without any feelings of jealousy, rivalry or upset. You are committed to being a team together.

Respect

Respectful behaviour – words and actions – also forms part of a good marriage framework. Politeness, and responses that have due regard for the feelings and rights of your spouse, are so important. Some people say, 'I just need to get things off my chest,' but that is not acceptable if verbal abuse is used. Shouting is verbal aggression. Couples who shout at each other, or a relationship in which one partner regularly raises their voice, will see the destruction of the marriage by creating a harsh relationship framework that will eventually undermine communication and closeness.

Respect is also a feeling of deep admiration for someone, elicited by the fact of who they are: your spouse, whom you have committed to love and cherish. Respect is a buffer that frames our conversations and monitors our behaviour, especially during times of marital conflict. Being rude or condescending, or swearing at your spouse, is highly disrespectful and never justifiable. Disrespect chokes marriage relationships.

What makes a picture frame?

Your marriage context, or picture frame, is formed by the elements you put into it and how you choose to maintain and nurture or neglect them. The elements mentioned above are by no means a complete list of features that make for contentment and a good marriage, but they are high up on the list of practices to continually work on.

8

The colours of God's kingdom culture

We started this book by welcoming you to our own marriage and the principles and practices that have undergirded it. We have attempted to craft our advice for those anticipating married life as an intercultural couple in a way that makes clear our Christian faith, but is applicable to people of all faiths and none. In this chapter, we are going to expand on the distinctiveness of our identity as Christians and what that might mean for your marriage. We will focus on the culture – the customs, behaviours and attitudes – that is taught to us in the Bible. Besides the two of us and our individual earthly cultures, we see this biblical culture as a third strand that is woven into our relationship which, we believe, binds us together more than any other piece of advice, counselling or intervention ever could. We will refer to this as God's *kingdom culture*, a phrase that Christians use to refer to the spiritual authority of God in our lives that is different from the temporal authority and culture that we have focused on so far. It permeates every aspect of our lives and gives direction to how we do life together and in community.

Our purpose in this chapter is, first, to be realistic about the Church's responsibility to preach the good news of Jesus for all people – married or single, of all nations and cultures – and to alert you to the possibility that your church may not always be as constructive or supportive as you would expect. (In Chapter 11 of this book we encourage you to reach out to supportive friends, mentors and leaders who are willing to act as advocates for your marriage.) Later, we reflect on the teaching of the Bible, which provides a pattern for loving relationships that are held in the hands of God.

Before we start, we also want to point you towards Appendix 2, 'God and intercultural marriage', which deals with the underlying hesitation that some people have about God's response to intercultural relationships. In our experience, God's warnings to the Israelite people about the ungodliness of intercultural marriage can cause confusion and be a stumbling block to those who love the Lord and read the Bible. By looking at a wide range of Old and New Testament scriptures in the appendix, we hope to make clear that God's response to marriage between people of different cultures is based on his desire for holiness and cultural practices that support godliness.

To begin this chapter, we start with a reality check. The Christian faith does not immunise men and women from the challenges of an intercultural partnership. Reading the Bible, going to church and professing faith – none of these are guarantees of a successful marriage for anyone. In fact, we would argue that if you belong to a community of Christians and call yourself a Christian, the struggles that you experience as an intercultural couple may be all the more painful. Criticism, racism and ignorance are, unfortunately, found in Christian communities, and whenever any person of faith falls short of God's call to love, acceptance and inclusion, it is all the more bewildering and saddening.

Culture clashes in church

We have known many culture clashes in churches. A Christian perspective does not mean that conflict is easily resolved, and neither does it mean that the voices of those involved will be tempered or reasoned. In our experience, negative and unfiltered responses from some church members and leaders can add to the challenges that couples face. We have found that a couple's

Christian conviction about the choice of their life partner is often not heard or considered. We have seen men and women from different cultures accused of dishonouring their parents or being harbingers of a curse on their family because of their disobedience. *Real* Christians, they are told, would obey their parents' wishes.

Sheila was told by her father that she was to leave the family home immediately if she went ahead and married Jamie against his wishes. Sheila came to stay with us in the weeks leading up to her wedding, because others in the church had been won over by her parents and she was facing a constant barrage of opposition. Jamie was an upstanding Christian man but was totally unaccepted by Sheila's parents and others in the church from a similar cultural background, because he was of Caribbean heritage and they were from an African country.

On the face of it, churches can look like confidently multicultural spaces, with people of different cultures often working successfully alongside each other at church events. It seems, however, that Jesus' Great Commission to his followers to 'make disciples of all nations' (Matthew 28:19) can unite Christians around an evangelical vision and a focus on those whom they hope to reach outside of the Church, while stubborn prejudices that exist between the nations inside the congregation are glossed over.

Intercultural couples preparing for marriage have to deal with the very real 'baggage' of longstanding, historical conflict and discrimination between cultures and ethnic groups, such as the Protestants and Catholics of Northern Ireland, Pakistanis and Indians, Africans and Caribbeans, black and white South Africans or the Hutus and Tutsis of Rwanda. There are many more.

'But she is not Ugandan! She's not even African!' shouted Jonah's aunt. 'How can she be the mother of the family, in the future, as she should be in our culture?'

This was a protest we encountered from a Christian couple in the church, against a lovely young Christian woman.

People groups that have historically clashed for socio-political reasons, for example, tend to have a legacy of wariness towards each other generations later, fuelled by historical learned prejudices and stories that endorse them. These historical prejudices are carried into churches and Christian communities. Such fissures remain unchallenged and dormant until the possibility of a mixed-culture union looms on the horizon involving someone they care about.

Les recalls ... I received a phone call one night from the mother of a young woman in our congregation. The mother was hysterical, and some of her anger was directed at me and the church.

'We've known you all these years,' she shouted. 'We trusted you to look after our daughter, and you have allowed her to do this! How could you encourage this relationship?'

When I managed to calm her down, I found out that Tanya had just told her parents that she wanted to marry one of our young elders – an African gentleman. Tanya's family were from the Caribbean.

Challenges can lead to growth

As it happens, all of the relationships outlined above have worked and are still working beautifully, because the couples concerned love each other, and they thought and prayed carefully about their union before entering into it. They also had a conviction that their marriage was part of God's will for their lives.

We saw how the unnecessary heartache, opposition and threats to these couples from Christian parents and others in their church community actually caused each partner to pray and look carefully at what they were going to do. The end result was that their resolve was strengthened, as was their commitment to one another and to God. We have seen challenges in intercultural relationships lead to the growth of good fruit. For example:

- you might pray more together
- there might be more dialogue and communication between the two of you
- you might gravitate towards those in the church who are 'for' you, to pray for and support you in practical ways.

We suggest a number of intentional steps that you might find helpful. They won't necessarily be easy or quickly achievable, but they are vital to enable you to move forward when you face difficulties. As we have said elsewhere, we encourage you to deal with what has happened. Don't just bury the issue. Allow yourself time to pause and reflect on your situation.

Acknowledge and talk about the hurt and negativity of the experience you have faced. Confide in a church leader or Christian couple so that they can help you process it and pray for you.

Choose to forgive those who opposed you in painful ways through their words and/or actions. This will release *you* from the people and experiences that have hurt you so that you can heal and move on completely. The people you need to forgive may still be entrenched in their opinion and opposition. You cannot change them, but you can help yourself by taking this step of giving forgiveness.

Subsequently, whether you choose to change church or to remain, by taking these first two steps, you will release yourselves to move forward in your marriage without reviving past hurt in your minds. Be prayerful and unhurried about any decision to move from your current church. It is important to know God's leading to make the best decision for you both as a couple.

Take some time together now to reflect on your church context(s).

- What response do you expect from your church family to your decision to marry?
- What encouragement and support do you anticipate?
- Who will this support come from?
- Who do you think might give you a 'cooler' response? Why?

It is very easy to hastily dismiss the person with the 'cooler' response as not being 'for' you. However, Scripture states the value of listening to all advice and concerns, and ultimately weighing them up before applying or discarding them. The book of Proverbs contains these words: 'The way of fools seems right to them, but the wise listen to advice. Fools show their annoyance at once, but the prudent overlook an insult … The words of the reckless pierce like swords, but the tongue of the wise brings healing … Truthful lips endure for ever' (12:15–16, 18–19).

- Given these scriptural words of caution, how might you prepare yourself to approach and have a conversation with people who are not 'for' you?

God's kingdom culture

Having acknowledged that humans fail and cause pain and hurt to each other, the rest of this chapter is designed to reflect on the teaching of the Bible as a pattern that Christians are meant to imitate.

When we use the phrase 'God's kingdom culture' we refer to the presence of the kingdom of God on the earth, outworking through and in human lives until Christ returns to establish his kingdom fully.

'Seek first [God's] kingdom and his righteousness' (Matthew 6:33) is God's instruction to us as children of his kingdom. Seeking to know and apply what God's kingdom rule in our lives should look like is fundamental to our success as individual believers. Citizenship of God's kingdom is radical in that it requires us to place God's desires (as expressed in the Bible) and influence at the centre of every area of our lives. If necessary, its requirements overrule our personal culture!

The Bible shows that God's kingdom values are an internal system that we should imbibe, as his Holy Spirit works in us, so that it will guide our behaviour. God's values are principles for us to live by and they filter our behaviour. Ultimately, our behaviour and attitudes conform and we resemble children of God's kingdom. As many commentators have observed, our goal is to live out the values of the eternal kingdom. For Christians, our challenge is to be primarily influenced by God's word in Scripture, and the kingdom culture that it embodies and promotes. These values include love (for God and for others), righteousness, justice, humility, forgiveness, obedience and stewardship.

Both partners of a kingdom couple will be on the same page in terms of commitment to prioritising God's will for their lives. In other words, you both desire kingdom character formation (the fruit of the Spirit) and encourage each other in this. Here are some of the ways to understand this kingdom identity. You could use this simple list to guide your reflection together.

- You have a faith in God.
- You nurture a kingdom-culture environment in your home by consciously welcoming God's manifest presence there.

- You aim for holiness as the standard that you live by personally and as a couple, and you desire to know God's perspective and leading in your lives (Proverbs 3:6).
- You invite the presence of God's kingdom into situations, through prayer (Matthew 6:10).

The extract below, from an unknown Greek writer in the second century AD defending the Christian faith from its attackers, goes some way towards describing the features of couples whose lives together promote God's kingdom culture. It is known as the Epistle to Diognetus and is abridged here:

> The distinction between Christians and other men does not lie in country or language or customs … They follow local customs in clothing, food and in the rest of life; and yet they exhibit the wonderfully paradoxical nature of their own citizenship … They marry like everyone else, and have children: but they do not abort their young. They keep a common table but not a common bed. They live in the world but not in a worldly way. They enjoy a full life on earth but their citizenship is in heaven. They obey the appointed laws, but they surpass the laws in their lifestyle … They are poor but make many rich … In short, what the soul is in the body, that the Christians are in the world …

Two millennia later, J. John and Chris Walley, in their book *Jesus Christ – The Truth* (2022), include this list of kingdom-culture personal characteristics described by Jesus in his teachings:

- integrity – Luke 11:13; 24:49; Acts 1:8
- consistency – Matthew 5:33–37
- prayerfulness – Matthew 6:6–13; Mark 11:22–25
- forgiveness – Matthew 5:38–42

- humility – Matthew 7:1–5
- servant heartedness – Luke 22:25–27
- a right attitude to wealth and possessions – Luke 12:33–34
- love for one another – John 13:34–35
- joyfulness – Matthew 6:25–34
- hopefulness – Matthew 6:10.

For many, a shared religious belief becomes one of the strongest components of their relationship. A firm commitment to living out Christian values can be an important enabler to a long and healthy marriage.

Where the Bible is the benchmark for a Christian couple's marriage it provides the kingdom-culture colours for each spouse to use on their canvas. Some kingdom-culture colours, according to the Bible, need to replace elements of our personal/family culture if they are not compatible with, or are contradictory to, our joint faith convictions.

Agreement, in terms of religious affiliation and commitment, is about going forward with a deeper sense of unity and life purpose, especially as Christians together. As we have already mentioned, Scripture says, 'Do two walk together unless they have agreed to do so?' (Amos 3:3). Walking 'together' in marriage is fulfilling when a couple have a shared sense of spiritual identity and look together to God for his direction for their lives.

Adopting God's kingdom culture means adopting distinctives from Scripture and living by them. These may override or replace other or previous values and behaviours. For married Christians from different cultures, cultural choices are made largely from what each person brings to the marriage (what's on their colour palette) but as seen through the lens of kingdom-culture principles.

Maureen and Sam had a lot of opposition to their marriage at the beginning, but this encouraged them to examine carefully their decision to marry and consider carefully how they would craft their marriage going forward. They knew that, first and foremost, they wanted to embrace biblical Christian principles for doing life together, since their union was founded on their shared love of Christ. Their key scriptural principles to live by were:

Leaving and cleaving – they kept family members at a safe distance, especially since many were not in agreement with their marriage, but they found godly counsellors for the wisdom they did not have.

Husbands loving their wives as Christ loved the Church – Sam used this principle often and demonstrated such respect for Maureen in words, attitude and behaviour, and they used it in relating to each other. They agreed that 'Do not let the sun go down while you are still angry' (Ephesians 4:6) was an important principle when they had disagreements.

Loving others – another important one that the couple worked on together, especially after the wedding when they began thinking about what family relationships might look like. They were intentionally forgiving and loving, because the Bible commands that.

Praying together was an important ingredient in their marriage, particularly praying for wisdom to navigate and respond to prejudice. They asked for God's healing when things were said or done to them that were wilfully hurtful. They prayed for more grace to be Christ-like when they didn't feel like it! They experienced God's help in these things when they prayed.

As time went by, they drew closer to family and endeared themselves to them by adopting and using some surface cultural practices at appropriate times. For example, Maureen learned, and now uses, forms of greetings in Sam's native language. She wears traditional dress when appropriate at family events and so on. She recently achieved the accolade of having more 'culture' than her husband!

They decided that they wouldn't move to either of their native countries unless they knew that God was leading them there. When they visited Sam's homeland, Maureen observed and realised what Sam had resisted bringing into their home from his culture – a male-dominated society, with low regard for women. Sam honours women and he treats Maureen with honour, partly because of his godly mother and grandmother's influence on him.

Sam and Maureen were clear that the prevailing culture in their house would be God's kingdom culture.

We've created a flow chart that could support you in your conversations around the kingdom colours in the artwork of your marriage. On paper, it looks rather cold and mechanical, but by its nature it reduces something emotive and complex to something much simpler. Try it!

God's kingdom-culture colours are distinctly vibrant and can cancel out or tone down counter-cultures if, as a Christian couple, you are intentional with the colour choice and brush strokes, just as Sam and Maureen were.

What is on your individual paint palettes?

God's kingdom culture has distinctive colours which are, in other words, scriptural imperatives for Christian living that should show through and affect our entire lives. They should colour our personal landscape and our marriage. In this section we will encourage you

Kingdom culture in the artwork of your marriage

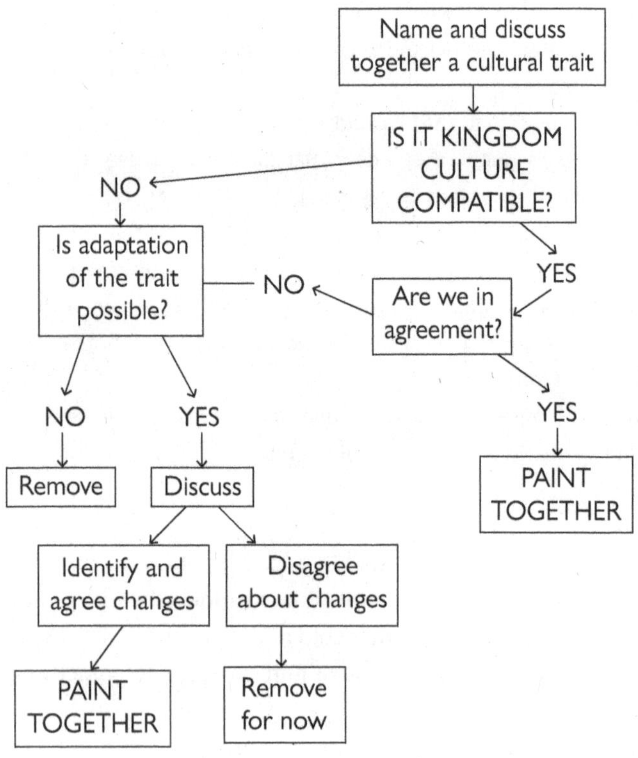

to discuss and compare your culture colours with the distinctive colours of God's kingdom principles, and consider the following questions:

- Do you have kingdom colours that are similar or complementary?
- Do some of your kingdom colours clash? (For example, 'Seek first the kingdom' means to prioritise God in all things. One partner may feel that going to church when on holiday is

essential; the other may feel that church attendance is off the agenda when on holiday.)
- Are any of your kingdom colours counter-cultural?
- Is it your kingdom identity that makes you feel uncomfortable with some cultural practices that have been family 'traditions' for years?

Leah and Luke were quite adamant at the beginning of their marriage that the prevailing mindset between them would be dominated by their shared Christian faith.

Since their marriage, most things from each of their cultural traditions and customs palette have had to pass through these filter questions first:

- What does the Bible say about it?
- Does it work for both of us?
- Does it maintain our unity?
- Will it work for our family in the future?

Luke and Leah both felt they needed to adapt some of their cultural traditions to make their marriage work, but even more, everything had to align with their commitment to God. They regard themselves as a kingdom couple first and foremost!

Denominational differences

Christian denominations have different cultures and practices, and these can add another layer of colour to your individual paint palette. Denominations express God's kingdom culture in different ways and use different language to mean the same thing. We hope to prepare you to identify these differences and be aware of how they might impact your relationship. We also want to encourage you to see the common 'spirit' behind different styles of churchmanship, so that you can appreciate and value the differences, while learning respect for the variety of traditions included in the Christian Church.

> *Louise recalls ... I have experienced the Lord's Supper in three different denominations. In each, the customs and practices were different.*
>
> *In the first, a silver goblet, a silver plate and a white lace tablecloth were used. The bread was cut into neat squares and the wine was non-alcoholic. In the second, I was given a tot-sized glass containing blackcurrant juice, and wafers were served on a delicate china plate. In the third, one large plastic cup of real wine was passed around the congregation, along with a wicker basket with chunks of bread.*
>
> *As my first church experience was the first one in the list above, any customs that came after it felt sacrilegious! I had to unpack this. Jesus said that we should eat bread and drink wine in remembrance of him (Matthew 26:26–28). This was God's kingdom-culture instruction. The choice of silver or wicker, juice or wine is just church culture!*

As you can see from the example above of the Lord's Supper (or Holy Communion, Breaking of Bread, Eucharist, Blessed Sacrament), there is a great deal of variety between denominational cultures. We include this illustration in order to get you to think about your own experiences and how these may influence your union.

If you and your partner come from different church cultures, take a moment to reflect on some of the differing practices and vocabulary.

Of course, it's not just the practice on its own that could cause tension. Longstanding practices lead to preferences, and preferences can lead to the belief that one way is superior to any other way of doing things. What you do, don't do or regard as acceptable is often learned from your church culture. Intercultural church marriages can highlight as many frustrations and anxieties as personal cultural differences.

Kingdom-culture norms: the example of prayer

We will now focus on prayer, because of its vital place in a Christian marriage. Committing to pray regularly together is important, because it helps to create a spiritual intimacy between you and encourages your growth together. Also, it helps to stave off opposition. Our marriages have a spiritual opponent who aims to subtly undermine and destroy every good marriage relationship. Our mandate in Scripture is to 'watch and pray' so that we can overcome the works of the devil (Matthew 26:41). We recommend agreeing how often you will pray together in a week, also when and where.

Below we will first identify the kingdom-culture norms concerning prayer – that is, the prayer instructions evident in Scripture for you to live by as a couple. After that we will look at the 'negotiables' of the different church cultures you have grown up with.

Prayer instructions in Scripture

These are just a few scriptures that can set the tone for your coming together regularly to pray for and with each other, about the things on your joint agenda.

Praying together and alone

There is no scripture that directly says that husbands and wives must pray together or for each other, so we need to look for kingdom-culture principles for direction.

Jesus prayed daily, alone, to his Father. That is worth emulating, because it draws us into a closer personal relationship with God.

Jesus said that when we pray, we should make time to pray in private and be honest and open with God (Matthew 6:5–8).

Praying to God together as a married couple is a 'prayer of agreement'. Jesus said, 'If two of you on earth agree [that is, you are of one mind, in harmony] about anything they ask for [within the will of God], it will be done for them by my Father in heaven' (Matthew 18:19). Agreement in prayer draws us closer to the ones we pray with; it creates a unity.

Praying continually

Jesus said we should 'ask', 'seek' and 'knock' (Matthew 7:7–9). This scripture suggests a continual persistent approach to God with our prayers.

Church cultures and prayer

Think for a moment now about all the learned church behaviour that we adopt naturally or we expect to see in church. We tend to do the same things in private prayer as in public (church congregation) prayer. Our prayer posture, prayer language and prayer content is usually very similar.

Selina Stone, in her book *Tarry Awhile* (2023), describes the experience of a Pentecostal church-goer encountering another church and prayer tradition for the first time:

> Silent prayer sounded like an oxymoron when I first heard it. I grew up in a church that liked words, and lots of them. We believed that God knew what was in our hearts, but we also really liked loud, passionate praying. Prayers included emotion, demonstrating that one's whole self was involved in that moment of intercession ... speaking in tongues was also an important part of prayer ... I had never imagined that silence in prayer was possible or even spiritually acceptable.

Les recalls ... I remember the first time Louise and I prayed together alone in my flat. Louise comes from a traditional, holiness Pentecostal church background. In her church, when someone said, 'Let us pray,' everybody stood and prayed simultaneously out loud.

One evening, after discussing wedding things and just before I took Louise home, I said, 'Let's pray first.' She agreed and I started to pray out loud. Louise immediately joined in, out loud. After a few seconds I stopped.

'Louise,' I said, 'if we are going to agree in prayer, we need to pray one at a time so that we can hear what the other is saying!' She paused, slightly embarrassed, then agreed, quickly realising that what I had said made good sense. I continued to pray, then it was her turn to pray as we stood holding hands in the doorway. So, ever since, that is how we've prayed together.

Consider how you pray together as a couple or, indeed, why you don't pray together. There might be unconscious discomfort, embarrassment or frustration to do with the different traditions you have come from. There may be things that you need to talk through and overcome or compromise on so that you can approach your heavenly Father together, in agreement. You each might have a different interpretation of how to pray, based on your own church experience. What constitutes 'regular' prayer for one person may not be so for another.

Jenny and Eric had different expectations about the baseline of prayer in their marriage. Jenny told Eric that she was concerned that they weren't praying together. Eric was surprised, pointing out that they always prayed together before leaving for church on Sundays.

When a couple discover that they have different expectations about the essentials, we have found that it is helpful to be prescriptive. You may consider this too rigid, but even if you only adopt it as a time-limited measure, it helps to set habits. We have sometimes given a couple written prayers as a scaffold to get them started in praying together. There are some suggestions for support that you might find helpful in 'Further reading' at the back of this book.

As a couple it is good to get comfortable with praying out loud in each other's company, simply so that you can join in and agree with the things that each of you says. It's much like a conversation between three people.

Your posture, language and liturgy are all negotiable, and you will each have good practices that, together, you can choose from and blend into your prayer rhythm as a couple. Praying together is a joint agenda of praise, worship and speaking to God that is separate from your individual prayer times.

Feeling awkward about praying together is often raised as an issue between couples, especially those of very different personalities and church backgrounds. Praying together to God is so good for your marital health, it is worthwhile pressing through the awkward phase to a place of feeling less self-conscious. Remind yourselves often that your appointment together is with God, and he doesn't compare your eloquence or theological prowess. He just wants you both near him, to talk with him in humility and honesty.

To illustrate the range of church cultures, we've included here a list of prayer postures, prayer language and prayer content from various denominations that are all permissible before God. There may be others that you can add. Which do you use? What do you feel uncomfortable with? Reflect on this together.

Posture	*Language*	*Content*
Standing	Seventeenth century	Liturgy
Sitting	Conversational	Reciting songs
Walking	Spiritual tongues	Reading psalms
Kneeling	Lots of silence	Praying Scripture
Head bowed	Meditative	Short-sentence prayers
Head raised	Out loud	Long prayers
Arms raised	Declarative	Spontaneous
Hands together	Formal	Short-sentence prayers
Palms facing up	Non-verbal	Informal

9

The first brush strokes

In this chapter, we want to think about your wedding day and the early months of your life together. The first brush strokes on your intercultural marriage canvas will appear at the wedding, so it's important to be intentional about what it will look like. It will be your first explicit statement and celebration of your union as husband and wife from two different cultural backgrounds.

We appreciate that some of you will already be married, but the principle of embracing both your cultures in significant celebrations is worth considering (baby naming ceremonies, for example), to acknowledge your heritage and aim to enjoy celebrating it with families and friends.

Weddings are full of vibrant colour – the flowers, the outfits, the table decor and so on. Weddings can also have lots of vibrant cultural colour. They are one of the few significant life events that are celebrated in most cultures, through various customs and rituals, to mark the important rite of passage of a couple moving into a legally, socially and religiously sanctioned life of union together.

In most cultures, wedding celebrations include traditions, customs and cultural practices involving the couple, parents and family members in a joyous 'union festival', which can last hours and sometimes days. With all of the interest and emotion around it, the declaration from one or both of the couple – 'It's *my* wedding!' – can be futile and often falls on the deaf ears of parents and family members.

In many cultures, the wedding is actually considered to belong to the parents and older family members. It is seen as the culmination of and prize for all their hard work and sacrifice in raising their child to adulthood. The wedding day is when they are able to watch them transition into a new phase of life, and this is a time to celebrate. Therefore, they want to be involved in the planning of it. The wedding, for many parents, is a proud display of achievement to all the family and friends who matter to them.

Culturally it is important for you both to appreciate this back story and the level of emotion behind each parental request and preference concerning the wedding preparations.

Pre-marriage cultural formalities and protocols

Your cultural consciousness and sensitivity will likely go down well with your future spouse and in-laws. Try therefore to maintain a good flow of communication about each other's expectations, even though you do not share the same cultural background. Appropriate observance of cultural protocols will send the message that you are trying your best, and it will consequently be appreciated by the family.

> *Les recalls ... We were informed that in the Nigerian tradition our son Jake should not approach his prospective parents-in-law to ask to marry their daughter. Instead, a senior male member of the young man's family was to make the first approach. We wanted to be sensitive to and appreciate the importance of this cultural tradition, so I arranged an appointment with my future daughter-in-law's father, observing the cultural values related to hierarchy and formality.*
>
> *With Louise, I visited their home, and we sat, exchanged pleasantries and ate together. Then I asked on Jake's behalf. The father seemed pleasantly surprised and was very approving. With that preparation done, our son was then at liberty to ask*

the father for his daughter's hand in marriage. This was the beginning of a good and mutually understanding relationship between our families.

The wedding guest list

In our experience, one of the biggest challenges between couples and parents at the start of wedding planning is deciding on the guest list. We have known parents get so annoyed with the decisions made by the couple that they have chosen to override these and print their own unofficial invitations for the friends they want to invite, regardless of the size of the venue!

Les recalls ... I was so upset when my daughter Lara told me how few guests I could invite to her wedding! This was partly because it created a serious dilemma for me, which she did not appreciate the extent of. I recalled all the people in churches where I had been the pastor who had blessed us as a family and Lara in particular. They had prayed for us, looked out for us, given us gifts over many years. And now I would have to tell these people that they couldn't come to our daughter's wedding.

One of the ways that we, as a family, got around this issue of who was to be invited to the wedding was to have an additional celebration. Both our son and our daughter chose to marry partners of Nigerian heritage, so on each occasion we all agreed to have two ceremonies – a Nigerian traditional wedding and a British wedding – managing carefully the numbers and cost of each. You too could think creatively about a second celebration if numbers become an issue. For us, the events were not equal in terms of size or formality or cost, but both were appropriately full of customs and rituals and joy, demonstrating the wealth of background culture that our families were celebrating.

The cultural detail of traditional weddings

Many rituals and customs can be involved in traditional weddings. As a Christian couple, it is important to find out the root and purpose of these to ensure they are aligned with your Christian principles and do not offend God. Also, each of you needs to feel comfortable with your involvement in any ceremonial rituals or requirements as a person from a different cultural background.

> *Louise recalls ... In the lead-up to his traditional wedding, we noticed that our son seemed anxious about something. He told us that he was uncomfortable with the ceremonial requirement of prostrating at the feet of his prospective father-in-law, as is the custom of young Nigerian men at their traditional wedding. We encouraged him to talk to his fiancée's family about it. They appreciated his concern and consequently waived this requirement. Our son also decided not to wear Nigerian traditional attire, but instead wore a jacket and trouser suit with a tie to match his bride's Nigerian outfit. He said this was to make the statement that he was a young Caribbean man marrying a Nigerian woman.*

We all agreed to a traditional Nigerian wedding for our son, containing rituals and ceremonies to acknowledge and join the two families. (Most African and Asian countries have traditional wedding ceremonies that pre-date the Western wedding model, and are still legitimate and embraced as a rich cultural practice today.) A list of gifts to be wrapped and presented at the wedding was sent to us by our future daughter-in-law's family. In discussion with her parents, we discovered the meaning behind each gift and together we agreed on the ones that would be appropriate for both families. For example, both families agreed that large sums of money would not be exchanged (token amounts only, in the spirit of the tradition, would be gifted) and alcohol would also be excluded from the gift list.

We wanted to embrace this custom of gift-giving and also use it to reflect our Caribbean culture. For example, one item on the list was a set of cooking pots. We exchanged this for a Dutch pot – a large, versatile, cast-iron cooking pot to be found in every Caribbean home. The thought behind this was that Caribbean meals would be cooked in their home, as well as Nigerian. Our son's fiancée embraced this.

For our daughter's traditional wedding, we added two blankets to the gift list. One was to represent warmth between them in their new family; the other was to signify Christian hospitality and 'spare-bed ministry' – an example we had modelled.

Families from different cultural backgrounds need to work together to make traditional weddings meaningful and celebratory for both families as much as for the couple. Your aim is for immediate and extended families to enjoy the cultural richness of your wedding day.

We want to encourage you to take the time to work with family to include cultural statements in your wedding, because both of your cultures are valuable and to be celebrated on such a special occasion. (We recall one couple of German and English heritage choosing to have fish and chips for the wedding breakfast!) Think about food, emblems, flowers, colours, dress, music and so on. Be culturally creative!

Our final word of advice about wedding preparations is not to burn bridges because of wedding plans. Acknowledge and appreciate that you and your parents are emotionally involved in the wedding and that these emotions may overflow at times and be expressed through requests and expectations. Therefore, be prepared to compromise on some things to ensure that the bigger picture – your married life – still includes people who are important to you both.

Harry and Taani knew that her mum was disappointed Harry was not from their cultural background. Being a widow and Taani being her only daughter, Mum nonetheless reluctantly attended the white wedding. Taani did not want a traditional wedding, and this added another layer of disconnect between Harry and his future mother-in-law.

Unbeknown to Taani, Harry had bought and wrapped several gifts for his mother-in-law. On the wedding day, during the first part of the reception, he had his groomsmen bring in the gifts and present them to her as he knelt before her, kissed her hands, humbly thanked her for her daughter's hand in marriage and made a speech about his commitment to her, the family and Taani. This gesture melted Mum to tears, and went on to soften her heart towards him in future years.

The colour of sex

Sex is a neutral colour, but it absorbs the colours and tones added to it from various sources over time, including deep-culture colours from your background and from later personal experiences. Ultimately, sex can look very different in each person's mind in terms of expectations and how you might respond physically and emotionally to it and the prospect of sexual intimacy in marriage.

Sexual intimacy is a big subject and there are many resources available that deal with the topic in more depth than we can. Our aim here is simply to highlight and get you to begin unpacking your own deep-culture influences and other experiences you've had, as they will inform your perceptions of sex and might affect your experience of sexual intimacy as a couple.

Let's first remind ourselves of some deep-culture definitions relevant to understanding sex in an individual's life and therefore what you might bring to the marriage canvas. These include values and beliefs that are shared community thinking about what is good or right, bad or wrong. They are perceptions about standards of behaviour considered important by a community. These affect our ethics, which are behaviours informed by a person's morals.

Sex in each culture is coloured by the values, beliefs and ethics taught and learned within a society, both explicitly and implied, by, for example, body language and even silence. A good starting point for looking at this topic might be to ask yourself what you saw, heard and felt about the subject of sex (including your sexuality as a boy or girl) from your earliest recollections at home, then outside of the home – for example in school.

The next layer of colour, on top of this deep-culture learning, comes from various sexual experiences that have impacted you. Together, deep-culture background learning and life experiences contribute to forming opinions, expectations, images and emotions that can affect your current perception of sex and ultimately your approach to the prospect of sexual union and intimacy in marriage.

Look at the word cloud below. You might find it helpful to reflect on your life in three phases: childhood, teenage years and adulthood. You could respond to the list of words by placing the most appropriate ones for you under each life phase, adding any other relevant words that are not on the list.

contraception ‘being a man’
experienced
‘being a woman’ defiled
masturbation anticipation regret
naive guilt shame
rape inexperienced unprepared
romance promiscuity penetration
careful taboo abuse nakedness
loved embarrassment
STD awkward pornography
pain virginity innocent
vulnerability
pleasure babies

The aim is to provide the starting point for a discussion between you both, about the values, beliefs and experiences that provide you with a colour on your personal palettes with regard to sex. Here is an example:

	Childhood	*Teenage years*	*Adulthood*
Person 1	silence abuse	secrecy pornography	contraception promiscuous
Person 2	silence romance	body shame anticipation	virgin

Whichever words are chosen need to be explained so that you both share an appreciation of your background culture and experiences. The discussion between you then might move on to how these experiences are likely to feed into your intercultural relationship.

Alternatively, you could choose three words that resonate with you (because they reflect your background culture or experience in some way) and that you might find helpful to talk about with your partner.

It could be that you need to address some aspect of your past by getting help from reading resources or counselling in order to be able to move forward as a couple in this area. As Christians, we are aware that while reflecting on and talking through this subject you might feel some regret regarding your past. If so, we want to say that self-condemnation is not a part of this exercise. The Bible tells us, 'Therefore, there is now no condemnation for those who are in Christ Jesus' (Romans 8:1). Any sense of guilt can be given up in exchange for the forgiveness and cleansing power of Jesus Christ. Isaiah 53:5–6 says of Jesus, 'He was pierced for our transgressions, he was crushed for our iniquities; the punishment that brought us peace was on him, and by his wounds we are healed … the LORD has laid on him the iniquity of us all.' We believe there is nothing in our past experience that cannot be overcome with God's help to allow us to move into a place of freedom and health, enabling sexual intimacy that is wholesome.

Trevor had carried a lot of guilt and shame related to pre-marital sex and pornography. Not sharing this with his wife – and, worse, not realising how these experiences shaped his perceptions of intimacy in the early part of his marriage – was unhelpful. For example, he consciously and subconsciously believed that intimacy was all about his needs rather than what his wife wanted and needed as well. His colourful sexual history had also led him to naively believe that he was sexually experienced. As a result, he put himself under a lot of pressure and an expectation that things should automatically be great, based on his 'experience'. It was a shock to realise that what he thought he had learned in the past, and the 'techniques' that he had practised, did *not* prepare him to understand his wife's body or her needs.

If sexual intimacy becomes an issue for either of you, and you become aware that it relates to background culture or later life experiences, it is important to keep talking, even if it feels uncomfortable. Sexual intimacy involves being physically and emotionally vulnerable to each other, so choose caring words and be gracious, understanding and non-judgemental in hearing what your spouse has to say, in order to avoid shutdown or conflict.

The 'Further reading' section contains a book that many couples we have talked to have found helpful.

The first year: making changes

Here we want to anticipate decisions that, in our experience, are commonly discussed and often acted on in the early stages of married life for intercultural couples. Our focus here is on change. Of course, you will have both made one of life's biggest changes at the altar but, for some, this change can lead to others. The two changes that we are going to discuss are changing country and changing church.

We'll come right out and say that in our experience, significant changes about which country to live in and which church to go to are often knee-jerk reactions. They can spring from the impulse to get away from what you have experienced before. Couples are also attracted to additional life changes after their union because of the thrill of a new adventure. For an intercultural couple, more so than for a couple who come from the same country of origin, there is always a real possibility of moving to one of the countries that their families come from. It's a viable option.

In the lead-up to a move from one country or church to another, the thought process may go something like this: *we have experienced difficulties in our current setting. People who are close to us have been set against our marriage. We have faced long-term opposition that has been wearing. Leaving this city/church behind would give us some breathing space to establish ourselves as a couple. We have had a long-distance relationship and now finally we can be together in the same country and/or church.*

We understand that it feels attractive to put the past behind you and start a new life together. However, making a knee-jerk decision is never a good thing. Listed below are some of the things to be aware of and discuss prayerfully before you make a decision to move from one country to another, or from one church to another, following your marriage:

- Are you *both* ready for this move? Some people relish change and others can't stand the idea. Make sure you talk through thoroughly how each of you feels about a new adventure.
- Will you be accepted as a couple in this new place or might there be further, different, problems that you will need to address?
- What adjustments will you need to make in the new setting? How will your roles and expectations change? What are the challenges for you as individuals and as a couple?
- What sources of support will you have in the new setting?

Big life changes can create pressures that you haven't anticipated. It may seem attractive but, in reality, moving to another church or country is another 'new thing' that you will have to work on and get accustomed to on top of living together as husband and wife. The move might become another 'task', another body of stuff to deal with. This has the potential to be quite a burden.

Changing church: a new Christian family

Changing churches can be a natural decision when you have attended different churches. Obviously moving so that you are both part of the same church is expected, and something would be wrong if you did not want to worship together. When preparing for a new start *for both of you*, then everything we have said above applies. Make sure that your foundations are strong before you add any more challenges to the early stage of your marriage.

Church culture differs between Christian denominations and also within denominations. When we moved from one Pentecostal church to another, we realised the congregations were very different from each other culturally. We had no idea what we were moving into. With hindsight we could have prepared ourselves better.

Think carefully about which church you should attend before making any move. Here are some questions to consider:

- What is your motivation for wanting to move?
- How culturally similar or dissimilar to your current place of worship is the church that you are considering, in terms of people and practices?
- Will you be able to fit into the new church family?
- Is this church a place where you can grow spiritually, individually and as a couple?
- What structures does the church have to facilitate your growth and support your marriage?

Approach this prayerfully and in conversation with each other. Weigh up the pros and cons, and discuss any honest reservations.

Changing country: a new cultural context

We know of a number of couples who have chosen to emigrate after their wedding. The book of Ruth in the Old Testament expresses some of the challenges of navigating a new culture. The story begins with Naomi leaving her home with her husband and two young sons to move to another country, Moab, for economic reasons. Naomi's two sons grow up and marry local women.

A few years later Naomi's husband dies, and not long after, each of her two sons dies, leaving her two daughters-in-law as young widows. Without any men to take care of her or her daughters-in-law, Naomi feels vulnerable in her cultural context, so she decides to return to her homeland. She thinks that going back to Judah would be better for them than remaining in Moab. The three women begin their journey, but Naomi stops and instructs the two young women to go back to their parents in Moab and feel free to marry again. One of them, Orpah, leaves, but Ruth, the other one, insists on continuing with Naomi.

In Judah, Ruth has a lot to manage, as she has given up her culture and all things familiar to her. She has to learn to function in a different country. Naomi is instrumental in guiding and instructing Ruth in the cultural traditions and customs of the Israeli people so that, as far as possible, she can stay safe, survive and thrive as a young foreign woman in an unfamiliar country.

The story has a lovely ending, and if you don't know it, you can read it for yourself! It gets us thinking about intercultural marriages, where one spouse agrees to leave their homeland to live abroad in the nation and cultural context of the other. It is very clear how much Ruth and Naomi needed each other in the new land. Naomi's initial decision to return to the safety of her people establishes her as a thoughtful woman, who was aware of the consequences of her choice of place, for herself and for her daughters-in-law. For Ruth, Naomi provided knowledge of the new context, 'ears on the ground' so to speak, with local information and guidance about how Ruth should behave in order to survive and thrive, economically, socially and personally, and ultimately make an intercultural marriage with Boaz.

Bringing a spouse to Britain, or going to live abroad with your new spouse, is a big decision to make – very different from going on holiday for a few weeks! Practically, emotionally and culturally, the experience can be exciting but also challenging for both of you.

We want to encourage thoughtful consideration of your reasons for moving to another country before you take such a step.

Work

Often the reason for the move is work related and you are motivated by the hope of a better quality of life, much like we saw with Naomi. A work opportunity may already be in place for one of you. If you have one job to go to but not two, what will the other person do after the period of setting up home has ended? If employment does not materialise, for whatever reason, how will your spouse maintain their wellbeing? Feeling swamped, imposed upon or isolated in a new or only partially familiar place can be overwhelming as time passes and can create a challenge to that person's individual identity, especially where there is no opportunity to connect with their own background culture and people who have a similar experience of it. If a pregnancy happens, how will this affect your work plans, your roles and expectations of each other? Ultimately, the extent and duration of the challenges will determine how well you settle as a couple.

Family and friends in the new context

Some couples have a strong desire to go 'back home' as a married couple. In practice, this means your family and friends have to learn and then accept your new identity. Importantly, they must recognise that your old, single life has ended and you have a new role now. This may need to be stated explicitly, at appropriate times, to family and friends.

Going home, therefore, may require lots of mutual care and attention to help one of you settle into an unfamiliar setting, and the other to settle into a role that is unfamiliar to family and friends in the local area. Socially and personally, your task will be to develop new relationships and establish a sense of identity as a married couple in the new context.

A new 'deep' culture

Together you will need to learn/teach and navigate the deep-culture norms of the country. This may mean that there is an imbalance between the two of you, with the partner who has the strongest connection to the new culture finding themselves taking the role of leader and tutor to their spouse. If there is less multiculturalism in the new context, this may have implications and mean that care and attention is needed to make sure that one partner does not feel alienated or marginalised.

The importance of your foundations

There are lots of possible configurations that can determine the outcomes of a move. We want to share just two important considerations for you to discuss as a starter, before a major move:

- Is your relationship in a good place, with a secure picture frame (especially, for newly-weds, in terms of a strong friendship) that will anchor you as you manage the potential challenges and curve-balls that will come in this season of change, when everything is new in a different country?
- How will you prepare culturally? Will there be people close by who can help you with the unknown cultural nuances? In the Bible story of Ruth and Naomi, Ruth went out to work after having been informed by Naomi of where to go, what to do and not do, because she recalled how things worked from her previous life in Judah.

10

Painting on your canvas together

Deciding what you want and don't want in your own marriage is a good starting point for creating a work of art. Discussing together what you want to perpetuate and promote in your marriage is important. It is also a good idea to address negative experiences, abuse and trauma. When we are not intentional, it's very easy to slip into, and repeat in later life, the negative attitudes and behaviours that are observed and imbibed in our early years.

> *Les recalls ... When I was seven years old, my dad walked out of our home for good. I was unable to articulate the pain and turmoil in my young mind then, but I now know that I experienced trauma, grief and bereavement. Shortly after this, I vowed to myself that if I ever got married and had children, I would never leave them – a vow I have followed through on intentionally, with God's help. I have consciously tried to be a good, faithful husband!*

Being intentional about the positive experiences you want to carry through or establish in your marriage requires self-awareness and deliberate actions and attitudes.

The example of physical affection

Some would say that physical affection has a lot to do with how you are wired personally. This does play a part, but most of it relates to cultural roots. It stems from what we believe is acceptable behaviour in public and private, and from attitudes learned about explicit demonstrations of (sexless) physical affection and touch beyond early childhood.

Often during our marriage courses this topic takes up far more time than is allocated, because it is such an emotive subject. It draws both men and women into thinking in detail about their experience of affection from their earliest recollections of childhood to their current experience in marriage. Appropriate, sexless, physical affection is culturally dictated. It is largely learned through observation and experience with parents and family.

In group discussions there is always the unanimous chorus of 'I knew my parents loved me' before an outpouring of accounts of how physical affection within the home did not necessarily endorse or accompany that sense of being loved. Age and gender factors also affect how much physical affection is experienced.

On the other hand, some group members, from different cultural backgrounds, describe their childhood and upbringing in a 'touchy-feely family', seeing and experiencing hugs, kisses, hand-holding and so on. The cultural difference element of the group discussions is always the most enlightening for all. Generally, it becomes apparent that couples have never spoken together about their experience of affection. Individuals have made assumptions about the other's background on this topic – usually that their experience was similar. Some experience frustration or disappointment around this subject because of a lack of affection in their marriage, especially after the honeymoon. But as couples talk and listen, and realise the cultural roots of their differences, we have helped them consider the possibility of unlearning and adopting new patterns of behaviour to make their marriage work better.

Neither of us grew up in a physically affectionate home (love was experienced in other ways). In our marriage, therefore, we have been intentional about changing this – brightening the colours significantly, as it were, between us and especially with our children through to adulthood. We see hugs, kisses and words of affection as important ways of affirming, encouraging and demonstrating love in our family. This was not the case at the start of our marriage.

Louise recalls ... Early in our marriage, Les and I struggled with our differences and needs relating to this subject of sexless physical affection. Although culturally, in my upbringing, physical affection was sparse, in my personality type I had a strong need for sexless physical affection. Les, with his background and gender role expectations, regarded himself as 'not the affectionate type'. We finally came to a place of wanting to work this out together. After much discussion, I realised that part of his intransigence was to do with not knowing how to change! I wanted to help him change, to help our marriage and future family.

Bringing about change

We came across a theory that was particularly helpful in demonstrating how we could successfully work through the process of personal behavioural change. This was Noel Burch's Stages of Competence model (1970) and we have shared it often in our marriage course. The theory refers to four stages of self-awareness and skills acquisition that help to make a couple aware of how they might experience progression in changing their own behaviour.

At times, one or both of you may need to look at how you can change to bring about synergy. Cultural behaviour change, which is supported by both of you, can be a slow but very valuable process for your marriage if you persevere with it.

The four stages in the process of behaviour change suggested by Burch are these:

1 *Unconscious incompetence* – at this first stage you are ignorant of what you are doing, its effects on your relationship and its origins.
2 *Conscious incompetence* – you become aware of specific behaviour that needs to change (included or excluded), but don't know where to begin or what to do to change or make it better.
3 *Conscious competence* – you actively decide to learn and practise new behaviours. This stage is the most awkward and frustrating, because often the behaviours feel unnatural or forced and calculated. Sometimes you may get it wrong or forget to do it!
4 *Unconscious competence* – after conscious, repeated practice (and some failure) the new behaviour begins to feel less awkward and more natural. You have achieved behaviour change. It feels and happens more spontaneously, such that you no longer have to remind yourself because it has become a subconscious behaviour.

We return to the example of physical affection in our own marriage journey to illustrate this.

> *Louise recalls ... Les was not the hugging kind. He said this often in our early days of marriage, as if by saying it he could make my need for hugs and physical affection suddenly disappear! Les was unconsciously incompetent in terms of being physically affectionate. He also didn't know and hadn't thought about it as an issue in our relationship until I raised it.*
>
> *We talked about him not being the affectionate type. I needed him to understand that I was an affectionate person and it was important for my wellbeing and my sense of our personal intimacy. Les, being the caring person he is, agreed to work on demonstrating physical affection more often (aside*

from affection that accompanied sex). With my encouragement and support, he worked his way through the stages of behaviour change mentioned.

In terms of conscious incompetence, Les initially protested that he was unable to change because of the way he was brought up, especially when he felt it wasn't working. However, as his attitude changed, we managed and worked through the awkwardness of the conscious competence stage. Often during this stage, I would jokingly stand in front of him, right in his personal space, and remind him it was time for a hug! 'Make this one at least ten seconds long,' I would say. Or, 'Repeat after me...' and give him a nice slow body stroke! He would laugh, but he got the message, and then came a time when the reminders were no longer necessary.

Les now hugs without prompts – he is an unconsciously competent, physically affectionate person (overall) and I love it!

You might find it helpful to consider this process in addressing other behaviours you would like to see appear consistently in your marriage, or indeed disappear. Agreement about what you would both like to see is the first step; this step also encompasses a positive attitude towards change itself, and this will motivate and help you to persevere. Acknowledging that you will not always get it right, or that things may lapse at times, will help to avoid undue guilt or a sense of total failure. Finally, grace and humour can help to get you through, especially at the most difficult stage of conscious competence, when the new behaviour feels forced and unnatural.

Be new culture creators

We are at liberty to be culture creators! Being a culture creator means that you can paint with new colours on your marriage canvas and use deliberate, positive strokes.

Allow us to reiterate some of what we have mentioned in Chapter 8 regarding kingdom culture. The Israelite people had been an underclass in Egypt for generations. When God finally got them out of Egypt, he had a job to get Egypt out of the Israelites! God had to re-construct their values, attitudes and behaviour in many important areas of life, so that they no longer resembled the Egyptians in their way of life, and not least in their religious practices. God stated explicitly what they should and should not do as individuals, families and a nation going forward into their new life of freedom. God told them his expectations of them in terms of morality, beliefs, customs, upbringing, notions of cleanliness, food, dress and so on. He gave them a new culture.

We suggest that this example invites us to liberally 'create' culture and counter-culture in our marriages and families. This can be a challenge to couples, especially in societies where there is discrimination and elitism. Some ethnic groups are looked down on and treated unfairly to the extent that they subconsciously have low expectations of themselves in some areas of life.

We have known couples who deal with societal negativity by adopting (among other things) counter-cultural phrases taken from Scripture or motivational speakers in order to encourage and maintain their family self-esteem. One such 'watchword' could be derived from God's address to the Israelites – a small nation surrounded by more powerful nations – when he promised them his blessing and provision if they remained faithful. In the book of Deuteronomy we read, 'The LORD will make you the head, not the tail. If you pay attention to the commands of the LORD your God that I give you this day and carefully follow them, you will always be at the top, never at the bottom' (Deuteronomy 28:13). In the context of marginalisation, then and now, a couple or a family might remember words like these, supported by prayer and actions, to encourage a mindset that keeps a consciously chosen culture alive.

You can also incorporate valued cultural practices within your marriage canvas that are taken from ethnic groups that are different from yours and your spouse's.

Les recalls ... Some years ago, Louise and I travelled together to Ghana and observed that certain dishes were eaten with your fingers. I had experienced this on a previous trip, but this was Louise's first encounter with the custom. Neither of us were accustomed to this from our own cultural background, but we had a go!

On other occasions we noticed also that couples would share a bowl of food placed evenly between them and use their fingers to eat from the same bowl. We loved the apparent intimacy of this shared meal – sitting close, each taking a portion of food from the plate and leaving enough for the other. During our holiday times in other countries we have often adopted this practice, buying a meal and sharing it in this way, taking pleasure in the closeness that it requires as we prefer one another's needs.

It is okay to look at the people in your cosmopolitan environment and make judgements about new colours and the new experiences that you might want to include to enrich your marriage and family life together.

Define your colours

Agreeing that you want a particular cultural norm to become evident in your marriage and family requires that you talk not only about the norm (the colour), but also the extent of its presence (the shades of that colour) and what it might look like in situ (how it will sit in the context of other life choices and your family).

Imagine you are choosing a new carpet for a room in your home. You agree on the colour – let's say blue – and your partner goes out to buy what you need. You are content to stay at home and not go to the carpet shop, because you are confident that your partner knows what shade of blue will suit the room and that your taste is for an understated, soft blue. Meanwhile, at the carpet shop, they are choosing a highly patterned carpet with multiple shades of blue!

As we have suggested before, a useful way to think about each cultural trait, and the extent of its impact or importance to you and in your marriage, might be to consider each trait on a spectrum of colour shades. Like the colour cards in a paint shop, the same colour has many different shades, from pale to brighter and deeper.

Look back at the colours of your upbringing

Most aspects of surface and deep culture can be considered in terms of colours and shades of colour. Test out the usefulness of this approach in your own relationship with the following practical exercise.

To begin with, look back at the cultural experiences in your upbringing, such as beliefs, traditions, attitudes and so on. Imagine a colour spectrum – something like the colour charts we've already referred to. Each shade has a number, 1 to 5. Number 1 is a pale shade, meaning you don't adhere much to the value or behaviour, whereas number 5 is a strong, dark colour, meaning that you strongly adhere to the value or behaviour. We've attached the following values to the colours:

1 This has no meaning for me	2 I am neutral on this	3 I have positive memories of this	4 This has influenced who I am today	5 This is part of my identity

Then take it in turns to choose a cultural trait that was important when you were growing up – for example, domestic cleanliness or gender role ideas. (You could use the deep- and surface-culture characteristics outlined in Chapter 2.)

Each partner should try to explain the number they have assigned to that cultural trait. Perhaps you can give some examples that illustrate your experience and why you have placed that cultural trait alongside that depth of colour. What emotion or level of energy was attached? Are there fond or uncomfortable feelings attached to the behaviour or custom?

Other questions you could ask include:

- Do I want more of this in my home?
- Do I want less of this?
- Can it be reproduced in our current cultural context in a slightly different colour?
- Would I like our children to experience this or not?

You are evaluating the past by looking back. Comparing each other's experience of the same cultural norm is an important part of this process. Seeing cultural differentness or similarity in your past experience is enlightening as you begin to make choices in your future together.

> *Louise recalls ... Just before Christmas and Easter in my home, my mother was always struck by a cleaning fever that all of us as children had to be a part of! It included washing and changing all the curtains and cleaning everything in the house that could be cleaned. 'Ready for Christmas!' or 'Ready for Easter!' she would say. For us children, this was a nightmarish time. I have never inflicted this on our children!*

In many non-Western cultures, academic prowess is considered an important cultural value (largely because it is a potential route out of poverty for an individual and a family). Being academically able therefore is applauded, but the negativity that can be poured on a less academically able child can be quite demoralising in some communities and families.

As a couple from different cultural backgrounds, you might both opt for the same shade of colour, but talking about how each of you experienced a cultural norm is also important and may determine how and when you will apply it in your marriage.

We have seen tension between couples when one partner subconsciously resists embracing a cultural norm without articulating the depth of their negative experience. If the other partner's experience was joyful and affirming then, without evidence to the contrary, they are likely to assume that their partner feels the same.

Look forward to the colours of your marriage

The next step is to look forward together as you consider the same cultural trait. What do you want it to look like in your marriage? What shade will it be on the spectrum? What does that shade mean to each of you? For example, you may both have a strong religious belief, but for one of you, your expectation is that church attendance is only for important occasions and you can watch church services online the rest of the time. Your spouse, however, may expect to pray together regularly, with weekly church attendance and involvement in church activities mid-week.

This careful looking forward is about checking to see that our cultural palette resembles the other's, or is complementary, so that we work together well on the canvas.

Be creative

In many nations, traditional family gatherings entail wearing items of clothing made from special fabrics of particular designs, especially for family events such as weddings, parties and funerals.

Joe was of Nigerian heritage and Jane of Caribbean. They knew that special events in Joe's family required a new special outfit in the family colours. This was fine for Jane in the first few years of marriage, until finances became tight. Joe felt they needed to keep up with the family expectation, but Jane was now concerned about the expensive fabric and the cost of a tailor to sew the designs. Also, the style was invariably such that it could not be worn again casually.

Joe and Jane talked this through to form a course of action that they agreed to adopt as a family, for themselves and their children. The wider family were informed and eventually came to accept it. They would buy a small amount of the 'family fabric' and make accessories, such as scarves, belts, rosettes or hats, to wear with plain-coloured items of clothing that they already had in their wardrobe.

Creatively changing cultural colours to make your marriage work is something that others can get used to eventually. Think of other family traditions that can be creatively tweaked and applied to acknowledge and honour, but also be sensitive to, your marriage and family needs.

Colourful language

Language, we think, is one of the most vibrant colours on the culture palette, but so often couples ignore it or are afraid to embrace it and be intentional about whether or not to use it as a way to relate to each other as a couple and, later, as a family.

It is said that familiarity breeds contempt, and many times when we have spoken to couples about the importance of maintaining their native language and subsequently teaching it to their children, we have found that the response is often lacklustre.

The issue for some is which language that should be. If yours is an intercultural marriage in which one or both of you have a native language, the question arises about which language to converse in at home. Invariably the default language becomes English, because it is known to both of you. We want to encourage you to think a little more about language choices.

We observe many intercultural families in which the children are never taught either language of their parents proficiently and, as a consequence, the main language at home becomes English because it is most convenient. That is not an intentional, conscious choice, but when these children become adults, many of them regret their parents' decision. More and more people are coming to realise the importance of language to a person's heritage and personal identity. In the global village we now live in, languages are a vital currency. People are more likely than ever before to travel or move to other countries for work or leisure and need a level of fluency to manage.

In our experience, the suggestion that partners learn each other's language and encourage its use in the home is met in one of the following ways:

- It is a chore to learn another language.
- It is a potential threat, because it highlights our difference.
- It means that I will be giving up my cultural space to embrace a language that won't necessarily make me more accepted by my spouse's people group.

Nonetheless, we want to throw out a challenge to you that is likely to reap rewards in the long term for each of you and your future children. Research stresses the benefits to children of learning another language. Early second-language learners have been shown to have improved brain and memory function and greater creativity. Never underestimate the incredible value of family dining-table talk – talking around a shared meal. This is when children develop their ability to take turns and follow a discussion, present their own ideas and listen to others. It has a massive impact on their self-esteem and debating skills. As parents, we steered and encouraged these family meals, thinking of them as 'talk times' with our children. We saw the benefits of this as our children grew. Table talk in at least one of your native languages would make it a culturally rich and affirming experience for your children.

Les recalls … We had invited Kofi and Sofia for dinner and a catch-up. They had been married for a year and still glowed with the joy of each having just moved in with their best friend! Kofi and Sofia were of Ugandan and German heritage, respectively. They had done a lot of talking about their backgrounds and how they would like to do life as a couple and as a family in the future.

They had decided that Sofia was going to teach their children to speak German fluently at home. Kofi said he was happy with that, but we questioned whether they had thought through how he would be excluded from this and how that would affect an inclusive family dynamic.

We encouraged Sofia and Kofi to look again at the language used in their home. Thinking ahead to the time when they hoped to have children, we reminded them that young children's minds are incredibly versatile and they are able to learn more than one language at a time. We know of a couple whose young grandchildren speak English, German and Portuguese fluently in their home and they are both under five years old!

We talked about Kofi's 'lost language'. He was born in the UK to Ugandan parents, but was never actually encouraged to converse in their Luganda language. As an adult, he has limited understanding and speaking ability in the language. This limits his intimate interaction with the wider family.

> *As we talked and ate, Sofia shared that she had grown up in a village in Germany with her mother and in recent years had come to live in London. Interestingly, Sofia pointed out that her spoken German had noticeably deteriorated since living in London and not conversing with Germans. Her mum and friends back home would point this out to her whenever she returned.*

We appreciated why Kofi wanted his children to be fluent in German, especially since he could not teach them Luganda. We suggested slightly different configurations for them to consider. Kofi could learn to speak German. He could use an online language learning course and, of course, learn through conversation with Sofia. For the present this would be a valuable learning experience for Kofi and it would also help sharpen Sofia's fading language skills. In the future, Kofi could then lead and contribute to table talk with his future children in a way that would not be possible if he did not learn to speak German. We also talked about the value of language 'immersion' through visits to Germany, and tuning in to German TV.

Language is a surface-culture topic, but as you can see, it is not shallow. It has, potentially, a far-reaching impact and is worth thinking through carefully. Kofi and Sofia left our home, we hope, appreciating the challenges and importance of learning each other's language and applying themselves to learning their first languages more proficiently.

It comes back to the idea of being intentional. We recommend that as a couple you have a conversation about the short- and long-term implications of being at least bi-lingual as a family. Talk about the potential benefits and losses of any decisions you make in this regard.

- Do you use your shared native language at home but speak English outside the home, with the intention of teaching your children the same?

- Where each of you speaks a different language, what choice will you make with future children in mind?
- Will you intentionally drop both native languages and speak only English at home?
- Will you teach each other your native language, then in the future teach your children both languages?
- Will you teach your children one or other language fluently (and your spouse)?

We hope this chapter has reminded you about the choices and creativity that are part of being intentional about the cultural colours of your marriage. Some of your choices will require reflection, and others may benefit from practice; some will arise from memories and nostalgia, others from the joy of looking ahead.

Part 4

GOING FORWARD

11

Sources of support for intercultural marriage

All married couples need support and encouragement at some point. Couples with the added dimensions of pronounced intercultural difference may need extra support, sometimes in the form of advocacy. An advocate is someone who will stand alongside you and support you as you express your views or tackle difficult issues.

In this section, we will offer our thoughts on what good practice looks like for intercultural marriages that need support. We will be addressing those people you might turn to for support. These could be people who have a formal or informal role in your church as supporters of engaged or newly-wed couples – for example, church leaders and pastors, mentors and those who lead marriage preparation courses. At the same time, however, we wish to alert you as a couple to the importance of seeking support. As we've said, all marriages need support at one time or another. Please don't hold back from asking for specific support when you need it.

Church, pastoral and marriage preparation leaders

The word 'multicultural' essentially refers to different cultural groups existing in the same space but largely functioning separately in a state of mutual tolerance. 'Intercultural', however, suggests a coming together, an interaction and mutual respect in the coexistence. So, what we often label multicultural is not what we imagine it to be. Where there is mutual appreciation and exchange between the variety of cultures in a community, that is, we think, intercultural. This is not meant as a play on words but rather for clarification; intercultural relations are, we believe, enlivened multiculturalism. For more on our definition of 'intercultural', please see Chapter 1.

On the face of it, a multicultural church looks more biblically acceptable than a segregated church or a predominantly monocultural church. A multicultural church can look as if it has people of every tribe and nation under its roof, and its leaders might boast of many different nationalities in their congregation. The problem is, however, many church leaders have little understanding or appreciation of their congregants' backgrounds or cultural norms beyond the 'surface' evidence. Often, multicultural churches are just that – lots of people from different cultures with little knowledge of each other or little interrelationship beyond the superficial. Jesus' words recorded in the Bible tell us, 'By this everyone will know that you are my disciples, if you love one another' (John 13:35). We believe this 'love' relates to a depth of relationship that is inclusive, knowledgeable and respectful of cultural differences and histories.

So, when Christian boy meets Christian girl in a multicultural church setting, leaders who are uninformed beyond the superficial will be of little help in intervening if there are family challenges related to them choosing to marry, and they will be unable to help couples manage and navigate cultural differences with informed sensitivity.

Our first pastorate was in south London, a multicultural church of young families from a few African countries and some older British folk from different parts of the UK.

Les recalls ... After my first year in post, I felt that culturally I didn't really know this varied group of people, especially those from the African continent. We had the same skin colour, but I knew they were different from myself in many respects

> *– different from Caribbean people on the whole – and they brought a unique specialness to the congregation that I didn't fully appreciate just by talking to them at the end of a church service or visiting them in their homes. So I decided to sample the cultures of my members by visiting some of their countries of origin. I visited and stayed in the homes of repatriated church members in Nigeria and Ghana, and attended their churches.*
>
> *These experiences opened my eyes to a whole new understanding and appreciation for these church members. They valued my interest in them and my willingness to step out of church and into their 'home' world, and this created a stronger bond between us. I also saw a new sense of liberty develop in the church as I challenged folk to be their authentic selves and express this in worship in the way they did in their home country.*
>
> *These visits paid huge dividends years later when there were issues that had cultural roots and required some understanding of backgrounds and cultural protocol in addressing them.*

We were grateful that Les had this opportunity and privilege to go and visit other countries to see and learn first-hand. We appreciate that this is not always possible. Leaders might therefore consider other ways to get beyond the facade and surface culture of congregants by being intentional about developing genuine personal relationships with individuals and families. When this framework is in place, questioning and sharing become accepted ways of understanding and appreciating difference, and embracing it in fellowship.

Second, we would hope that a leader would read about and research other cultures. Most church leaders will readily research and take courses to establish their understanding of a theological subject, and we believe that this is just as important! Reading relevant articles about the history, anthropology and sociology of the people group they are in fellowship with can be enlightening. They should ask questions to verify and clarify understanding.

When you, as a mixed culture couple, approach a church leader to get married and the fact of your cultural difference is ignored during marriage preparation, this can feel isolating and awkward, like an elephant in the room! If there are protests against the marriage from parents and, by contrast, silence from your church family, this can leave you, the couple, with an extra task to navigate alone, unnecessarily. We describe our own experience of isolation and lack of support in the early years of our marriage in the Welcome section of this book.

It is commonly said that love is blind. A supportive church leader has a responsibility to Christian couples to help remove the blindfold. They can do this by encouraging couples to begin to think through their differences and similarities and the potential impact of these for each partner within the relationship, and in their wider networks of family and friends.

Here is an outline of what we have tried to do as church leaders to support couples like you preparing for an intercultural marriage. You might want to consider asking for some of these interventions for your own situation when approaching your leader.

1 We have been prepared to offer a temporary safe space in the event of extreme hostility or homelessness due to the decision to marry.

> *Les recalls … Zara was glad to be offered our spare bed because it gave her a chance to clear her head and be out of what had now become an intimidating environment. While she was with us, up until the week of the wedding, we encouraged her and prayed with her often, and helped as far as possible with the practical wedding arrangements.*

2 We have prayed and provided some wisdom and discernment about the way forward for a couple in terms of timings, approaching parents together, deciding on a wedding date and so on.
3 We have met and talked regularly with couples, posing scenarios to encourage them to consider their intercultural marriage 'package'. How will they celebrate it and how will they approach the possibility that there will be uncomfortable bits for themselves and, in the future, for their children?
4 We have provided pre-marriage counselling or pointed a couple in the direction of a course that included cultural self-awareness.
5 We have tried to connect couples with other mixed culture couples who are welcoming and prepared to share about how they manage their relationship.
6 We have met with parents to listen to and respond to their concerns, while standing in support with the son or daughter. It is the leader's job to ask questions to unlock a parent's thinking, attitudes and, if relevant, prejudices, particularly if they are Christians. Scripture has many examples of intercultural married couples. The apostle Paul's instruction in the Bible, 'Do not be yoked together with unbelievers' (2 Corinthians 6:14), is the only scriptural basis of an argument against marriage. If such inequity is not the case, and if in every other respect the couple are mature, compatible and love each other, then the church leader should become their champion!
7 We have encouraged parents to be forthcoming in asking questions to gain clarity about the cultural background of the other side of the family so that they could begin to appreciate the cultural nuances of their future son- or daughter-in-law.
8 We have informed ourselves through reading and research. We have also asked questions and allowed individuals to let us

know the extent to which the cultural norms we had learned about applied to their particular situations.

Intercultural marriage mentors

We often talk about the importance of what we sometimes call 'mentor couples'. These are people who are not church leaders but they are trusted by couples and prepared to invest time and energy into someone else's marriage.

Outside of the times when we were church leaders, we have supported and helped engaged and married couples in whatever ways we can. We would describe our main giftings in this area as transparency, hospitality, prayer and advocacy. Below are some of the gifts that we believe enrich and sustain those delivering mentoring or marriage preparation.

Transparency

We are open and honest about our own relationship so that other couples can see a 'real' marriage. The backdrop to this is our own experience of church settings where there was a culture of silence and a level of pretence around marriage issues and challenges. As mentioned briefly at the start of this book, in our early years of marriage we became very aware of Christian marriage 'facades' and found this very unhelpful in trying to figure out who to approach for help in our marriage and how to know if what we were experiencing was normal or not.

We choose to talk to and share information with couples about how we have managed in our marriage – our joys and challenges. We want to be a help to newly-weds by being open and honest and real about our relationship. Couples then feel more able to approach us about their issues, knowing that we understand.

Hospitality

As the posters, mugs and prints have it, hospitality is just opening your home the same way you open up your heart. When we get caught up with concern for a person's wellbeing, it is natural to want to open our home and table to them.

> *Louise recalls ... When we first married, Les and I were at two different ends of the hospitality spectrum! In my home we never had people come to stay over, not even close family. In Les's home, there was often an openness to stop-overs, and the accommodation of foster children made his home a more open and sharing environment.*
>
> *I quickly came to realise that hospitality is not about being a brilliant cook – I never have been that – but rather having an open door, table and heart for people God wants us to serve. Nothing fancy appeared on our table, but there was lots of warm and welcoming conversation around it. What we came to call 'spare-bed ministry' was also a part of our repertoire when we felt it was needed. I would add that because our children grew up with hospitality as a significant cultural norm, they also now show hospitality.*

Prayer

We pray often for the couples we are responsible for. Prayer is not the least we can do; it is the most. This is our encouragement, especially in some of the tricky situations that couples face. To us, every single marriage matters. We are so aware of the importance of one person or couple being available to another. We believe that God uses each of us to help other people appropriately. This can have a profound and lasting impact on them, with a ripple effect into families and future generations. Therefore, being used by God to save just one marriage is success. Prayer and partnering with God is fundamental to that success.

Advocacy

An advocate is a person who can be another set of eyes to look at issues that are rooted in the different cultural backgrounds of the partners or their wider families. Many times we have sat with couples to listen and discern what is going on between them, trying to identify the root of the difficulty. If culture does have a part to play, we help them to recognise this. Addressing cultural norms is not easy and often not achieved immediately or quickly, but with lots of grace and a plan of action it is possible, and necessary, for the sake of their marriage.

When there are rumblings and challenges to do with cultural misunderstanding, prejudice or discrimination, godly advocates – an objective third party – can speak up and help couples to navigate their responses appropriately with regard to different cultures and God's kingdom culture.

To be a worthwhile help, in this area as in any other, mentors need to ask questions and do their own research while walking alongside. Often, we have been told by couples that just being there, standing with them and re-stating what they are saying, is the best support we could provide. Our due diligence involves praying and informing ourselves so that we are clear about all the factors involved.

Our starting position as Christian marriage supporters is always God's kingdom culture. What does the Bible say about the issue? Without taking the words of God out of context, are there any biblical principles that God wants us first and foremost to live by? If so, then that is the ground we need to stand on as Christian advocates and ensure that the couple understand this, so they also make life adjustments, if necessary, in line with the word of God.

Appendix 1
A pre-marriage questionnaire (designed with an awareness of cultural differences)

This questionnaire is another resource that you might find helpful in the run-up to getting married or as part of a marriage preparation course. It provides a selection of topics and questions that you could consider independently and then discuss together. In the marriage preparation sessions that we lead, we would normally go through each topic with a couple, elaborating on it with further questions to tease out each person's cultural colours. We encourage you to seek out someone, or another couple, you feel could support you in a reflective conversation using this questionnaire. Alternatively, if you have not yet participated in a marriage preparation course, you might be able to include it within the sessions.

The questions under each heading, and the cultural considerations that follow them, are the bare bones of the questions we would use to get couples to think about their personal background culture, God's kingdom culture and their exposure to other cultures – all of which may affect their answers. Importantly, it is an opportunity for each partner to flag up points for further discussion about how they might consciously choose to do life together on their shared canvas, going forward.

Relationship goals

- Why are you getting married?
- What do you as a couple want out of life?

- Do you think your relationship will change after you are married?
- What do you think you will be doing in thirty to forty years?

Cultural considerations

- Which examples of married life have you observed and what conclusions do you draw?
- If any of these relationships are long-term marriages, what have you observed about them in particular?
- Can you talk to any of these couples to get their wisdom and advice?

Household tasks

- How are you going to divide up the household chores?

Cultural considerations

- In your family home, who was expected to do certain household chores? List them and discuss the list.
- Who cleaned the toilet most often? Who put out the bins? Are you aware that these examples are likely to affect your way of doing life at home unless you are intentional about your behaviour and expectations regarding these tasks?

Spirituality

- How often will you pray together when you are married?
- Do you think faith and spirituality are important in marriage? In what ways?
- Which church will you attend and what are your reasons for choosing it?

Cultural considerations

- Faith and spirituality can be nominal or dynamic for each of you, or somewhere in between. To what extent are you as a couple complementary in this respect, especially if you have come from different church backgrounds?

Finances and goals

- Should you have a joint bank account?
- Are you a spender or a saver when it comes to money?
- Do you want to set a budget?
- Who will be responsible for making sure bills are paid on time?
- What are your financial goals?

Cultural considerations

- Has your approach to your finances been informed by observations, instructions or training from a significant adult in your life? If not, what has influenced it?
- How has your past affected what you do now?
- Who managed the finances in your childhood home?
- What financial expectations were there in your childhood home?
- How might you merge the best of what each of you has experienced in relation to financial management in your future home life?

Children

- Do you want to have children?
- How long should you be married before having children?
- What if you can't have children?
- How do you feel about adoption?
- What kind of parent do you think you will be?

Cultural considerations

- What are the unspoken expectations about having children in your families?
- What is your observation of experiences of childlessness in the family?
- What strategies and cultural experiences would you want to emulate in your own home while raising your children?
- What would you want to rule out and why?

Conflict

- Have you had any recurring arguments?
- Do you handle conflict well?
- How are you different in the way you each handle conflict?
- Do you think your differences will create problems in your marriage?

Cultural considerations

- What did serious conflict look like in each of your homes?
- Do you think your way of dealing with conflict is similar to, or different from, the way you saw conflict dealt with in your earlier years?
- What does 'handling conflict well' mean to you in terms of actions and communication?

Sex

- What are your hopes (perhaps as yet unspoken) about your sexual relationship?
- Are there issues from the past that will influence your ability to enter into a healthy sexual relationship?
- Are there resources, support or counselling that would be helpful in order for you to be ready to begin a physical union?

Cultural considerations

- What place does sex have in your culture?
- Are there positive or negative associations that you need to intentionally include or exclude?

Appendix 2
God and intercultural marriage

God is concerned about culture, because it profoundly affects how a person or community thinks and behaves. When God took the Israelites out of Egypt, he knew the next task was to take Egypt out of the Israelites! Many of the lifestyle practices of the Egyptians were unacceptable to God. Their immorality, pagan worship, attitudes, witchcraft and so forth offended God's standards of holiness and right living. God named these cultural norms and commanded that they be discarded and replaced with his holy values and practices.

In Exodus 20, God sought to change the Israelites' way of living after their departure from Egypt when he introduced them to the Ten Commandments. These commandments encapsulated what God expected of them moving forward.

Alongside the Ten Commandments, God also gave other more detailed laws. Some of these were new for an emerging nation; others addressed some of the abominable practices they had adopted while living in Egypt – for example, how servants should be treated (Exodus 21:1–11); how fights should be judged (21:12–27); how to deal with trespassing animals (21:28–35); various moral principles (Exodus 22:16–31); Sabbath rest in relation to agriculture (Exodus 23:10–13); holy annual feasts (23:14–19); regulations about the ark of the covenant, the tabernacle and the priesthood (Exodus chapters 25–28); what to do about diviners (divination was popular among the Egyptians) (Deuteronomy 13:1–5).

Some of the defiling practices – 'abominable customs' – that displeased God are listed in Leviticus 18:1–30. The verses specifically point out that these are the things that the people of Egypt, and the people in the land where they were going to, practised; most of which related to perverse sexual practices.

Intercultural marriage in the Old Testament

Culture in Scripture is an important corollary to Chapter 8 of this book, where we focus on God's kingdom culture as a shaping influence on our own marriage 'culture'. Our research on intercultural marriage, as referred to in Old Testament and New Testament references, is intended to be an introduction to God's stance on the subject and an interpretation of his reasons for objecting to such marriages.

Several times in the Old Testament God mentions nationals whom he specifically warns the Israelite people not to marry. God's objection was to do with their cultural practices, which he knew would draw the people away from following him.

God's expectation for marriage is that the two 'become one flesh' (Genesis 2:24b). A joining of lives includes sharing cultural practices: values, beliefs, religious practices and so on. And rightly so. However, many of the practices of the nations living around Israel were abhorrent to God. God warned the Israelites of the consequences of adopting these practices before they entered the promised land. We're now going to look at the key Old Testament verses on this subject.

Deuteronomy 7:3–7

> Do not intermarry with them. Do not give your daughters to their sons or take their daughters for your sons, for they will turn your children away from following me to serve other gods, and the LORD's anger will burn against you and will quickly destroy you. This is what you are to do to them: break down their altars, smash their sacred stones, cut down their Asherah poles and burn their idols in the fire. For you are a

> people holy to the LORD your God. The LORD your God has chosen you out of all the peoples on the face of the earth to be his people, his treasured possession.

Having had a measure of success settling into the promised land, Israel was warned again not to intermarry if they wanted God to continue to help them with their land conquests.

Intermarrying contributed to Israel's catastrophes. In the book of Ezra, all of chapter 9 highlights the catastrophes that Israel experienced because of intermarrying with foreigners. Again, it is the ungodly practices of the foreigners that are emphasised, especially in verses 11–12. Failure to desist from intermarrying could lead to Israel's total annihilation (verse 14).

1 Kings 11:1–13

Despite his impeccable wisdom, Solomon did not stay away from foreign women as God commanded ('You must not intermarry', verse 2). The result? God tore the kingdom away from him and gave it to his subordinate, as he said he would in verse 11. Again, it wasn't the foreigners themselves whom God had a problem with; it was the fact that they turned God's people away from him (verse 2).

Judges 3:5–8

The Lord tested the Israelites to see if they would obey him, but they disobeyed and intermarried with various groups. As a result, they went into captivity for eight years.

> The Israelites lived among the Canaanites, Hittites, Amorites, Perizzites, Hivites and Jebusites. They took their daughters in marriage, and gave their own daughters to their sons, and served their gods. The Israelites did evil in the eyes of the LORD. They forgot the LORD their God and served the Baals and the Asherahs. The anger of the LORD burned

> against Israel so that he sold them into the hands of Cushan-Rishathaim king of Aram Naharaim, to whom the Israelites were subject for eight years.

Nehemiah 13:23–27

When Nehemiah was putting things in order for the rededication of the Temple and the people, he noted things that he knew God was displeased with:

> Moreover, in those days I saw men of Judah who had married women from Ashdod, Ammon and Moab. Half of their children spoke the language of Ashdod or the language of one of the other peoples, and did not know how to speak the language of Judah. I rebuked them and called curses down on them. I beat some of the men and pulled out their hair. I made them take an oath in God's name and said: 'You are not to give your daughters in marriage to their sons, nor are you to take their daughters in marriage for your sons or for yourselves. Was it not because of marriages like these that Solomon king of Israel sinned? Among the many nations there was no king like him. He was loved by his God, and God made him king over all Israel, but even he was led into sin by foreign women. Must we hear now that you too are doing all this terrible wickedness and are being unfaithful to our God by marrying foreign women?'

The people were intermarrying and the prophet chastised them for this, noting how this was causing them to lose some of their own culture (they could no longer speak their own language). If the wisest king (Solomon) was brought down by this, he said, why did they think they could come out unscathed by sinning in the same way? Commitment to God was intricately linked to separation from the foreign people around them.

Are there any examples of intercultural marriage being permitted or accepted by God? Yes, there are. Let's look at some of those instances and God's response or involvement in them.

Moses and Zipporah

In Numbers 12, Aaron and Miriam speak against Moses because of the Midianite woman Moses has married. A foreign woman. One could argue that Moses had married a foreign wife before he led the Israelites out of Egypt, so God had not yet laid down the injunctions that they should not intermarry. More importantly, though, this Midianite wife, Zipporah, did not turn Moses away from the Lord (at least, there is no record of it).

Salman and Rahab

Salman was a Jew and Rahab was a prostitute from another nation – one of a few survivors from Jericho, if you recall. She and her household were spared during the destruction of Jericho and became part of the people of Israel (Joshua 6:23–25). Effectively, Rahab left her culture and background and adopted those of the Israelites and their God. Maybe this changed commitment was what qualified her to be part of the lineage of David and the Messiah.

Boaz and Ruth

In the book of Ruth, chapter 1, we read that Ruth was a foreigner who also aligned herself to the family of the children of Israel when she left Moab to live with her mother-in-law.

As with Rahab, her name is prominent in the genealogy of Jesus, showing that God can use intercultural marriages for his glory (this is in the Old Testament and may be seen as a foreshadowing of God's acceptance in the New Testament of all people from whatever nation).

Intercultural marriage in the New Testament

In the New Testament we see life for people of all ethnicities dominated by the rule and institutions of the Roman Empire. International trade and the movement of people groups under the Romans resulted in many more mixed households. Slaves were transported to other nations to serve. Work and education exposed people groups to other nationals. In Scripture, Timothy's parents were a mixed culture couple and, no doubt in the historical context, this was not uncommon. We note the similarity here to the recent trends that accompany today's globalisation. We read in Acts 16:1 that 'Paul came to Derbe and then to Lystra, where a disciple named Timothy lived, whose mother was Jewish and a believer but whose father was a Greek'.

Nowhere in the New Testament does God instruct anyone to reject a potential marriage partner on the grounds of ethnic origin. Instead, Scripture encourages the choice to be based on the person's commitment and devotion to God. We are told: 'Then Peter began to speak: "I now realise how true it is that God does not show favouritism but accepts from every nation the one who fears him and does what is right"' (Acts 10:34–35).

Nowhere in the New Testament is God's partiality or acceptance of a person linked to a command not to marry a foreigner. This is different from the Old Testament, where the command to not marry a foreigner is set out in clear terms, along with the reasons for the command.

What can we conclude?

In both the Old and the New Testament, God is more concerned with character and holiness when it comes to lifestyle and marriage. God's concern with good character and holiness can also be seen (and extended to marriage) in the verse that speaks about not being unequally yoked with unbelievers: 'Do not be yoked together with unbelievers. For what do righteousness and wickedness have in common? Or what fellowship can light have with darkness? What harmony is there between Christ and Belial? Or what does a believer have in common with an unbeliever?' (2 Corinthians 6:14–15).

In the New Testament, when marriage is talked about it is often in relation to faithfulness and treating each other with love, often comparing the marriage relationship to Christ's union with the Church (see, for example, Ephesians 5:23–29; Colossians 3:18–19; I Peter 3:7). This is what we refer to in Chapter 8 as adopting God's kingdom-culture values in marriage.

So, does culture matter to God? Yes, it does. In the Old Testament, we see God wanting to craft a new culture for his new nation, Israel, that he has brought out of Egypt. In the New Testament, we see Jesus endorsing God's cultural mores and putting forward a counter-culture to the ways of the Jewish people at the time – God's kingdom culture. Being selective of cultural practices that endorse good character and holiness is God's priority, especially for Christian marriages.

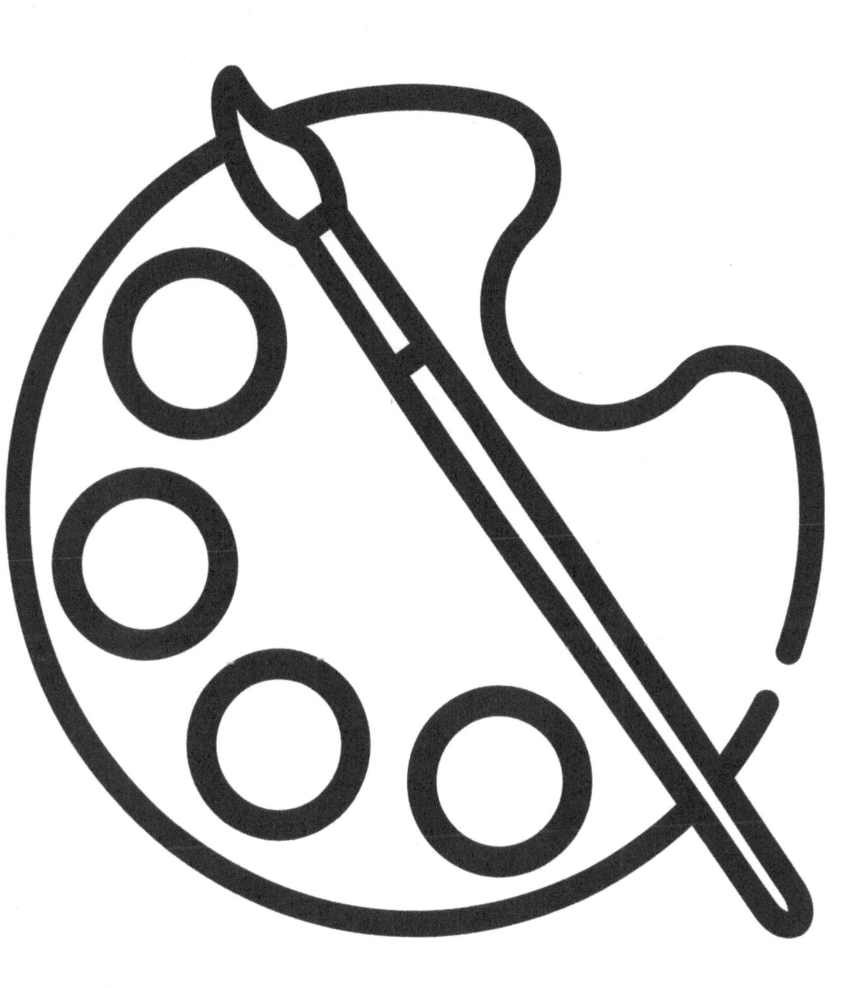

Further reading

Johann Christoph Arnold, *Why Forgive?* (New York: Plough Publishing House, 2008).

Francis Chan and Lisa Chan, *You and Me Forever: Marriage in light of eternity* (San Francisco: Claire Love Publishing, 2014).

Tony Evans, *Let's Get to Know Each Other: What white and black Christians need to know about each other* (Nashville: Thomas Nelson, 1995), chapter 7, 'The biblical mandate for unity'.

J. John and Chris Walley, *Jesus Christ – The Truth* (Rickmansworth: Philo Trust, 2022).

Stormie Omartian, *The Power of a Praying Husband: Book of prayers* (Eugene: Harvest House Publishers, 2014).

Stormie Omartian, *The Power of a Praying Wife: Book of prayers* (Eugene: Harvest House Publishers, 2014).

Clifford Penner and Joyce Penner, *Restoring the Pleasure: Complete step-by-step programs to help couples overcome the most common sexual barriers* (Word Publishing, 1993).

John Powell, *Why Am I Afraid to Tell You Who I Am?* (Grand Rapids: Zondervan, 1999).

Selina Stone, *Tarry Awhile: Wisdom from Black spirituality for people of faith* (London: SPCK, 2023).